CRITICAL ACCLAIM
FOR *TRAVELERS' TALES*

"The *Travelers' Tales* series is quite remarkable."
—Jan Morris, author of *Journeys*, *Locations*, and *Hong Kong*

"For the thoughtful traveler, these books are an invaluable resource. There's nothing like them on the market."
—Pico Iyer, author of *Video Night in Kathmandu*

"The *Travelers' Tales* series should become required reading for anyone visiting a foreign country who wants to truly step off the tourist track and experience another culture, another place, first hand."
—Nancy Paradis, *St. Petersburg Times*

"...*Travelers' Tales* is a valuable addition to any pre-departure reading list."
—Tony Wheeler, publisher, Lonely Planet Publications

"I can't think of a better way to get comfortable with a destination than by delving into *Travelers' Tales*...before reading a guidebook, before seeing a travel agent. The series helps visitors refine their interests and readies them to communicate with the peoples they come in contact with...."
—Paul Glassman, Society of American Travel Writers

"This is the stuff memories can be duplicated from."
—Karen Krebsbach, *Foreign Service Journal*

"Like having been there, done it, seen it. If there's one thing traditional guidebooks lack, it's the really juicy travel information, the personal stories about back alleys and brief encounters. The *Travelers' Tales* series fills this gap with an approach that's all anecdotes, no directions."
—Jim Gullo, *Diversion*

SAFETY
And
SECURITY

★
★ ★

For Women
Who Travel

TRAVELERS' TALES GUIDES

SAFETY
And
SECURITY

★
★ ★

For Women
Who Travel

SHEILA SWAN AND PETER LAUFER

TRAVELERS' TALES, INC.
SAN FRANCISCO, CALIFORNIA

Travelers' Tales: Safety and Security for Women Who Travel
By Sheila Swan and Peter Laufer

Copyright © 1998 Travelers' Tales, Inc. All rights reserved.
Printed in the United States of America.

Travelers' Tales and Travelers' Tales Guides are trademarks of Travelers' Tales, Inc.,
San Francisco, California.

Cover and interior design: Art direction by Kathryn Heflin; design by Susan Bailey
Cover illustration: © Michael Surles, watercolor painting of travel gear
Page layout by Patty Holden, using the fonts Berkeley, Copperplate, and Savoye

"A Stroll on the Beach" by Rebecca Aaland published with permission of the author.
Copyright © 1998 by Rebecca Aaland.

Distributed by O'Reilly and Associates, Inc., 101 Morris Street,
Sebastopol, California 95472

Printing History
October 1998:   First Edition

ISBN: 1-885211-29-5

TABLE OF CONTENTS

INTRODUCTION

Travellers sometimes buy jewels and bury them in their
flesh. They make a gash, put the jewels in, and allow the flesh
to grow over them as it would over a bullet. The operation is
more to succeed if the jewels are put in a silver tube with rounded
ends, for silver does not irritate. If the jewels are buried without
the tube, they must have no sharp edges. The best place for
burying them is in the left arm, at the spot chosen for vaccination.
A traveller who was thus provided would always have a small
capital to fall back upon, though robbed of everything he wore.

—*Francis Galton,* Art of Travel *(1872)*

No woman needs go to such extremes today.

Las Vegas, winter. As usual, I am writing late at night while
Peter dreams; he writes in the morning while I sleep. The hotel
is at the end of the strip, almost out of town—an adequate
low-cost place. Outside the room, I sit in the corridor rewriting the notes I took during the day.

My bones are cold, sitting in the unheated hall. I keep my
long purple wool coat on, a black angora beret on my head,
and thick socks under my thin leather boots. With a drink
from the bar, I'm lost in my thoughts.

Security guards periodically walk back and forth, squawking on their walkie-talkies. This is Las Vegas—house security
is in evidence even far from the famous casinos. I try not to
let them intrude on my work, but it's difficult, their radios
are noisy.

"A woman," one of them says.

I continue to write.

Soon there are two security men huddled down the hallway.

"Send a female," I can't help but hear one of them request over his radio. Now I'm a little interested in what trouble they're experiencing. A rowdy perhaps, down the hall, on the casino floor? I begin to write down what is developing around me for some future story.

Suddenly the two guards and a woman surround me, hovering over me. The woman looks menacing and her voice is demanding.

"What are you doing here?"

"Writing," I say, looking now to see if they carry guns. "Why? What's wrong? What's going on here?"

"That's what we want to know," she barks back at me. "Are you a guest here?"

I say yes and begin searching in my coat pocket for the key-card—just a strip of plastic with holes in it and no identifying hotel name or room number.

"What room are you in?" asks the demanding woman in a threatening voice. She too is in a hotel security guard's uniform.

"It's around the corner. I don't know the number."

"Don't move," she says. "What's your name?" The three of them stand over me like the guards they are.

"Sheila Swan," I say. "Sheila Swan Laufer. Look, whatever is wrong here, we can clear right up. I'll just go over to the room. My husband is in there."

"Don't move," is her response. One of the men is talking back and forth into his radio, saying my name. Irritation is combining with my surprise and initial confusion.

"I'm a guest in this hotel," I say. "Whatever is going on here is ridiculous…"

"We'll decide about that," the pushy woman interrupts me.

"Stay put."

The guard talking on the radio looks up at the woman and reports, "No Lanfer here, no Swan."

"No, it's L-A-U-F like Frank E-R," I say. "Peter and Sheila. Just go around the corner, first door on the left. He will be asleep, but he will answer. Please." I'm not sure if it's the cold or the encounter, but I realize I'm shivering, shaking.

"We don't disturb our guests."

"I'm a guest," I insist. "Just go over there."

"Don't move."

I sit there thinking and watching them. What if the computer failed? No Laufer would come up on their screen. Would I be jailed for vagrancy or trespassing, or just thrown out of the hotel? At least if I were just thrown out I could call Peter from a pay phone. For the first time in my adult life I feel completely trapped.

Now years later, as Peter and I finish this safety and security guide for women travelers, that Las Vegas encounter came back to me vividly, as a reminder that—especially for women—trouble on the road can come in the most unexpected places and from those strangers you tend not to regard with suspicion. In these pages we deal with all sorts of threats women face on the road: from foreign customs and prejudices, to potential rapists and robbers, from specific health and hygiene needs to the vagaries of dating fellow travelers. And while awareness of risk is important, equally important is the attitude you bring to it, and your own honest assessment of yourself as a traveler—strengths and weaknesses, nightmares and desires, past experiences, and dreams for the future. Safety and security are affected by real outside circumstances, but they can also be powerfully affected by your state of mind.

We hope this book will help women travelers find an important delicate balance: enough consciousness about safety and security to help you get home healthy and happy without raising your anxiety level so that the journey becomes an exercise in paranoia and avoidance of those things that make travel so rewarding, the unexpected, the new, the serendipitous.

The Las Vegas guard's walkie-talkie squawks again with the message, "Yes. Laufer. Room 1221."

"Oh. Are you Mrs. Laufer?" asks my captor. "Can you please show us your key? We'll take you to your room."

"I don't need an escort." I am angry.

Nonetheless the three of them follow me as I walk to the room and push the strip of plastic into the door.

"You understand, Mrs. Laufer, it is for your security that we make sure everything is safe here in our hotel."

I shut the door, hard.

On the other hand, they were just doing their jobs, no malice intended; all the more reason for the experience to serve as a reminder to me of the tenuous nature of safety and security on the road.

The advice in these pages offers specific and tested tactics and techniques to help you travel safely and securely. In all aspects of travel there is an element of danger and the information in this book will help you assess and reduce the risks to your own personal comfort level. However, there is no substitute—and never will be—for your own awareness and instinct supported by on-the-spot observation and information gleaned from locals.

Chapter One

BEFORE YOU LEAVE

The East looks to itself; it knows nothing of
the greater world of which you are a citizen,
asks nothing of you and of your civilization.

—*Gertrude Bell*, Safar Nameh-Persian Pictures *(1894)*

Consider the case of a friend of mine who was carefully preparing for her first overseas trip to come and meet me in Paris. Hers was a well-planned trip, and during her research she read some horror story about European Gypsies targeting lone women to pickpocket. She bought a money belt, satisfied that her funds would be safe tight against her body.

When she told her husband and mother about her clever purchase, they teased her relentlessly.

"How are you going to feel safe getting out your money while pulling up your dress?" her husband laughed, for she never wore jeans or slacks, her wardrobe consisted only of dresses.

What works for one woman does not necessarily work for another. We must each make our own individual checklists to ensure that our own customs and habits are accommodated.

Preparation for a long-distance voyage does not eliminate the opportunity for discoveries and surprises on the road. Every trip is full of serendipity. Planning ahead leaves you free of many unnecessary burdens and allows you more freedom to simply enjoy yourself.

One evening in San Blas, Mexico I climbed a hill for a better vista of an outstanding sunset. By the time I returned to the car, mosquitoes had taken enough of my blood to help someone in need of a transfusion. My traveling companion actually counted them as I scratched all over—he stopped at ninety-five!

Had I packed some Benadryl, I would have at least enjoyed some relief through the night. (And the sandflies in New Zealand can make Mexican mosquitoes feel like a gentle tickling, but that's another story.)

I am not a methodical person in the rest of my life, but before a long trip, I rely on no one but myself.

First I go to my doctor for prescriptions for cough medicines and antibiotics, and other basic medicines which might not be easily available at my destination—just in case I get sick on the road. I fill my vitamin box, adding a spare bottle of Wellness Formula—a cold cure-all I believe helps knock out colds and flus when they first strike. Wellness Formula is concocted by a company called Source Naturals in Scotts Valley, California.

One week before my departure date, I check the weather at my destination—information available in the daily newspapers, guidebooks, and the World Wide Web. Three days before I leave, my suitcase is packed with clothing that fits the climate. Two days before take-off, my carry-on bag is filled with all the things I'm convinced I cannot live without

I go to a travel agency and pick up itineraries for tours and excursions. I never go on those things—I don't like to travel with other people like that— but I pick up the brochures and see generally the direction they travel and where they choose to stop.

◆

Barbara Grosso, teacher

taking: extra contact lenses, my prescription for them, the stuff I use every night to wash my face. I leave this bag in my bathroom as I use the contents at home.

The day I leave, I simply place each of the things I use in my daily routine back in the bag as I get ready to go—toothbrush, toothpaste, hairbrush. This system ensures that none of my crucial daily tools are left behind.

And I aim for an afternoon flight, because I'm no morning person. Now that overseas flights require two-hour check-ins, I don't want to add to the stress of departure with worries that an early-morning rush might create some forgetfulness.

This is what I need to do to reduce the anxiety of preparing to leave home. Each person is of course unique in this way, but your goal is simply to be as tranquil as possible before you leave so that you arrive in better possession of your faculties.

You may already know a great deal about staying safe at home. Such experience and just good habits will serve you quite well abroad. But don't be surprised if you make mistakes and feel awkward as you adjust to new customs, languages, food, water, and time zones. Many travelers also experience loneliness and feelings of vulnerability that can come with being far away from home, family, and the familiar.

Tips

➢ Packing a destination-specific traveling medicine cabinet is well worth the trouble and expense. Most of the pills and sprays you'll want—the insect repellents and cramp relief compounds—that are available over the counter at

One of my cardinal travel rules: Invest in a pair of great walking shoes, and break them in before the trip. Comfortable feet mean less stress, less stress means I'm loose, light on my feet. I never wear thongs when I'm traveling—can't run in them.

♦

*Margaret Bradford,
photographer*

home may be harder, if not impossible, to find once you get on the road. High-potency vitamin C, for example, the type available at any U.S. health food store or chain drug store, is an unknown item in many European stores, let alone Third World markets.

➢ Ask your doctor to suggest and write prescriptions for medicines you may need specifically for the places where you are traveling. Get them filled at home, because the prescriptions may be invalid abroad. Keep the pills in their respective containers with the labels attached so that border guards don't suspect your vitamins or birth control pills to be illegal narcotics. (That's not as far-fetched as it sounds. Years ago Peter was held by the San Francisco police until he was able to convince them that what they claimed was peyote and LSD was, in fact, dried peaches and tapioca pudding mix!)

➢ A warm country can turn cold unpredictably. Bring clothes that can be layered easily to provide extra warmth. The lingerie sections of most department

Dress down. Use really ratty backpacks, don't buy Gucci or high-end suitcases because those are the ones that people tend to target. Friends who traveled in South America took local feedbags and put them over their backpacks to not have Western backpacks visible on top of buses. Speaking a few words of the local language, even if you don't really know it, will throw people off. My brother would say always check in with the local embassy and make sure to give power of attorney to somebody in case something happens. Take copies of your passport with you and leave copies with someone at home, it makes replacement easier.

♦

Maria Hudnut, exporter

stores stock thin cotton tops that add protection without looking like bulky underwear.

➤ A long black dress and some dressy shoes should be packed in case of a chance meeting with a diplomat who invites you to a reception at the embassy or if you get an unexpected invitation to a symphony concert.

➤ Remember to do the standard pre-departure steps at your house like stopping the mail and the newspaper. Let a trusted neighbor know you're traveling. Leave a light on or buy a timer that turns a few lights on and off at irregular times to provide a lived-in appearance to the casual observer who may be casing your place. Consider arranging for the grass to be cut or the snow to be shoveled while you're gone.

➤ If you live alone, it might be worthwhile insurance to bring along a friend or someone with a dog when you do return home after a long time away, just in case somebody uninvited is inside when you arrive. Leave a radio on tuned to a 24-hour news or talk station.

> Take earplugs. They create a sense of personal space. They abstract you from whatever is going on around you.
>
> ♦
>
> *Kay Ryan, poet*

➤ Leave a key to your house with family members, trusted friends, or neighbors. You may need them to go in and check on something while you're gone. And, if you lose your own keys during the trip, you won't end up locked out of your own house.

➤ Consider using a housesitter if you are going on an extended trip. Bad guys can tell if a house is not being lived in.

➤ Copy all your airline ticket numbers and airline phone numbers. Leave one with a friend at home and one copy packed separate from the tickets. If you lose your tickets or they are stolen, having those numbers and the itinerary will make it much easier to convince the airline to help you continue your journey.

➤ A photocopy of your credit cards and ATM cards will make on-the-road replacement much quicker and easier, and will make it faster for you to notify the companies if your cards are lost or stolen so that you will not be responsible for any fraudulent charges. On the reverse side of most cards is the company's emergency 800 number. 800 numbers can now be called from overseas for a standard toll charge.

➤ Passports, visas, and any requisite health certificates should also be photocopied and stored separately from the originals.

> Drink a lot of water before you fly and while you're in the air. You'll arrive in better shape, especially on a long trip.
>
> ◆
>
> *Lynn Branden,*
> *operations manager*

➤ If you want to reduce attention from strange men, wear a wedding ring and carry a photograph of your husband (or an ersatz husband) that you can show to persistent suitors. Another picture of the children at holiday time can be helpful too. Use anybody's children if you don't have a family.

➤ You don't need to replace your suitcase with a cardboard box, or your camera case with a brown paper bag, but— depending on the potential dangers of your destination— you may wish to use ordinary-looking luggage that does not call attention to your relative affluence or your femininity.

➢ Use luggage tags that close over your name and address—hiding them from the view of would-be thieves and con artists.

➢ Make some effort to connect with women at home who have roots in the countries where you'll be traveling. You can find them easily at places such as ethnic restaurants, language schools, and social organizations.

➢ If a meal is being served on your flight, order a fruit plate or vegetarian plate at least 24 hours in advance, unless you like airplane food—or pack your own meal. Chances are you'll feel better on arrival.

➢ Expatriates living in America can provide contacts for you in their countries of origin and offer all sorts of ideas for your trips, from destinations the guidebooks may miss to places that it might by worthwhile for a woman to avoid. In addition, such a connection can help you learn what subtle customs and practices to expect, information that can make quite a difference for the woman traveler in many parts of the world.

> If you're late, go straight to the gate. You can check baggage there.
>
> ♦
>
> *Heather Honea,*
> *graduate student*

➢ Bring a purse-sized flashlight and extra batteries for it. Hotels sometimes suffer power failures and you'll be happy to have your own light to see around the room and to help guide you out of the building.

➢ It is vital for your security that you are not burdened by your luggage. Although it may seem convenient if some fellow offers to carry your bags, better not to allow it unless you know him or are certain he's an official baggage handler. Make sure you do not pack more than you can carry comfortably for long distances. Never be forced to compromise your safety because your belongings are too heavy or awkward to lug by yourself.

➤ Pack two cases, one with your vital necessities and the other with the types of clothing and incidentals that you can just abandon if you need to escape quickly from a dicey situation. You can always replace your clothes.

➤ Always carry with you those things that you really will be inconvenienced without: passport, credit cards, cash, and onward tickets. Never wander around without your passport. It is your ultimate identification to foreign authorities and if stolen, your passport is worth thousands of dollars on the black market. That can make it quite tempting to an underpaid hotel housekeeper or bell boy.

> Be honest with yourself is another major rule of travel. If you're fat and out of shape, don't try to climb a mountain. If you're afraid of water don't go on a raft trip. If you hate spiders and snakes, stay out of the tropics. If you can barely tolerate domestic flying, don't fly in Africa or South America, where some very funky things happen with air traffic. If you get a bad feeling about getting on that crowded bus or rusted prop plane, or you saw the pilot's red-rimmed eyes, don't get on board. Trust yourself. It's like a muscle that needs exercise.

♦

Stefania Payne, marathoner

➤ Your purse should be a shoulder bag with a zippered closure. Always remember to close the zipper and hold on to the purse even if you wear it slung over one shoulder and across your body. Otherwise thieves in crowds can easily slash the strap and run with the purse or slit the purse itself and empty it of your wallet before you know you've been attacked. If you wear a fanny pack, avoid wearing it on your back where you can't see it.

➤ Bring along small unique presents to offer those who provide you with hospitality or assistance. If you work for a company that uses pens or pins or other tokens adorned with its logo for promotion, consider packing a handful of them. Similarly, simple tourist trinkets—even postcards— from your hometown will be well-received.

➤ To break the ice with children (and their parents), bring along a wind-up toy or simple game; if you play a small instrument such as a harmonica, Jew's harp, or penny whistle, be sure to bring it and use it.

➤ Snapshots of your belongings as you pack them will help you deal with an insurance claim if your bags are lost or stolen.

I never take valuable jewelry with me. I never take anything exotic or expensive. I take real basic stuff, and I behave the way I behave at home: I avoid dark places late at night, lock my car, watch my purse. I don't really change my behavior. However, because I'm interested in getting to know people, I'm actually more open to meeting strangers when I travel than when I'm at home. You don't have to give away the store, you don't have to tell everything about yourself, you just size people up. So my guard is down a little bit more in terms of meeting people when I'm traveling but up in terms of all my material possessions and feelings of personal safety.

◆

Francine Keefer, journalist

Chapter Two

EN ROUTE

Good-bye. If you hear of my being stood up against a Mexican
wall and shot to rags, please know that I think that a pretty good
way to depart this life. It beats old age, disease, or falling down the
cellar steps. To be a Gringo in Mexico—ah, that is euthanasia!

—*Ambrose Bierce, in a 1913 letter home*

———

No question I've been lucky in my travels. The worst
physical assault I received was a slap on my legs from a
crone in the main Mazatlan market. She was selling tiny
chairs with woven seats and painted backs.

"You whore!" she spat at me in Spanish as she slapped me,
"to walk around with your legs."

Nice-looking legs they were, at the time connected to a '60s
California mentality that never considered a woman should
cover them. I was lucky with that slap. Had I walked into a bar
where the men viewed me as a whore, my blond self might have
been in big trouble on that first trip to a foreign country.

That same afternoon I found a seamstress and some wonderful fabric. I paid her whatever she asked—I wasn't about to
waste time bargaining—for four dresses that came down to my
ankles. She sewed them on a treadle machine—all night, I
imagine, because they were ready the next day.

In most fundamentalist Islamic countries women are considered fast and loose if they walk around without being almost
totally covered. In many countries that are predominantly
Catholic, pants and an uncovered head are unacceptable for

women inside a church. Even a handkerchief will suffice in an emergency for a head cover. In some cultures even looking a man in the eye is considered an invitation, and in many, traveling alone is evidence that you are in fact a whore or at least a woman of low morals.

When you land in another country, look around and see what the local women are wearing. They will be your key to appropriate dress and behavior. The best survival rule is to keep your body covered until you are certain that you will not cause yourself or others problems by exposing too much skin.

Your arrival in a foreign place can be an important transition time, whether you are there for the first time or a veteran of many visits. The more tranquil you can be as you face the challenge of a new culture, the more alert you likely will be not only to potential hazards, but to opportunities. One technique is to close your eyes as the aircraft is descending, breathe deeply, and imagine yourself smiling as you encounter crowds of people, the babel of languages. Your life is about to change, as it always does on a journey. Consider avoiding the mad rush to the exit of the aircraft, and if your are seated toward the rear of the plane, take the time instead to rest, to compose yourself for the important moments ahead.

$\mathcal{T}ips$

➤ While waiting in line to go through passport control, don't hold your passport out in front of you with the easily recognizable American eagle shining out at every opportunistic man seeking an opening. Hold it against your immigration and customs papers with the eagle and "United States of America" side hidden. There is no need to advertise your citizenship to fellow travelers, some of whom may harbor deep prejudices against the U.S. or strange ideas about American women and see you as a potential target.

➤ Choose your traveling garb carefully—not too revealing, unless you want to court random romantic attention. Make sure it's comfortable for long flights and easy to release in cramped airplane toilet facilities. Shun logo t-shirts and other markings that make it easy for hustlers

I don't carry very much money. When I'm going through security, I always put the big bag first and my purse and computer last.

◆

Jennifer Beardsley, marketing director

to make an approach that can catch you off guard. Just as parents are warned not to send their kids around town with their names plastered all over their clothing, you'll find it easier to be in charge of encounters with strangers if they

aren't starting conversations with you based on the football team or saloon advertised on your shirt.

➤ At the airport and at borders, seek out other women (particularly Western tourists) coming out of the country you're headed for. Ask them for advice. Most women are happy to share information and knowledge,

I try to give myself plenty of time so I'm never in a rush, arriving or leaving. I also plan my schedule so I'm not forced to eat in the hotel restaurant and spend a small fortune because I'm afraid to walk outside.

◆

Liz Duffy, cataloguer

and these women are ideal primary sources. They can tell you from first-hand experience what worked for them and what you might need to worry about and avoid. They can offer up-to-the-minute tips on restaurants and night clubs. They may even have some names and addresses to share.

➤ Remember the buddy system. Even if you are traveling alone, you'll find opportunities to meet temporary buddies. Conversations with seatmates on a long plane ride can provide you with enough of a rapport and enough confidence to suggest sharing a cab from the airport, and other casual joint ventures. The stress of the initial entry into a foreign port can be eased with a companion.

➤ When possible, don't stash your luggage in the cab trunk in case you need to quickly leave the taxi.

➤ If your seatmate takes advantage of the close proximity of airplane seating to touch you inappropriately, tell the flight attendants immediately. They will find you an alternative place on the plane. Choosing an aisle seat puts you in a much easier position to leave an uncomfortable or threatening situation.

I always bring material to read, since airplanes are so often delayed. When I travel, I try to take some common medicines, like allergy pills or Tylenol, rather than think that I can get it at the next stop. It's better to be prepared.

♦

Vicky Su, accountant and business owner

➤ Tear your name and address off any magazines you bring from home to read en route.

➤ To reduce swelling ankles, wear shoes on the plane that slip off easily, and bring a sweater on the flight to compensate for the airplane air conditioning—sometimes brutally cold even during flights from one hot climate to another. Carry at least one pair of comfortable walking shoes and don't bother bringing along new shoes that are not broken in already.

➤ Take the time to learn just a few words in the local language. Even if you have no talent for languages, being able to say things like *hello, please, thank you, no, I have a disease, I am sick, I need a doctor, call the police,* and *I need help,* can be crucial. If you really can't remember them, write them phonetically on a card and keep the card with you.

➤ Other words that are important to understand are those that may be said to you, or may be on signs, and could cause you distinct trouble if they are ignored. *Stop, no, forbidden, danger* and *no photographs* are vital to know.

➤ You may well feel disoriented at the beginning of a trip— the new territory, the jet-lag, the change in routine. Try not to make critical decisions during the first few days of travel.

➤ If your luggage is lost, report it to the airline before you leave the airport. Much lost luggage just missed the flight and shows up on the next one. Usually the airline will send it to your hotel as soon as it arrives for no charge. Sometimes first class and tourist baggage comes in on

When I'm traveling with my children, I enforce a "no sweets" rule. Everyone stays calmer that way, and we all arrive a little less frazzled.

◆

Larissa Mendez, mechanic

different carousels, so look at the carousels used for first class passengers' baggage even if you travel economy. Before you file a lost luggage form, check all carousels from your plane. A distinguishing mark on your suitcase, such as a piece of yarn or sticker that means something to you, makes it much easier to locate on the baggage carousel.

➢ If a genuine emergency occurs and you must return home immediately, many airlines will go out of their way to accommodate you no matter how restrictive your ticket.

➢ To avoid the vulnerable look of a woman standing around in the airport or the main square, guidebook in hand, searching for a hotel, book at least your first night's room in advance. It may cost more than you need or want to pay, but it is worth the security of knowing you'll be off the streets while you adjust your senses to being away from familiar home territory. If you book directly with the hotel instead of using a reservation service or a travel agent, you may get a discount that will more than pay for the long distance phone call. Always get the name of the clerk you speak with and a reservation number so that if there is a question about your accommodation when you arrive, you have a contact. And always ask to see the room before you take it. Some nice-looking lobbies are the front for dreadful little rooms.

> I roll most of my clothes up so they don't get wrinkled, and I put in enough underwear and socks in case I have to stay over a few extra days.
>
> ◆
>
> *Margaret Chaika, pulmonary rehabilitation coordinator*

➢ Consider packing a product called a travel sheet or sleep sack. It is an easily packed cotton or silk bag to sleep in on the chance that you end up in a hotel with sheets that don't meet your standards for cleanliness. You can also use it as an easily-washed liner for sleeping bags.

➤ When you reach your accommodations, put a hotel business card into your pocket and purse. If you're out and about and a language barrier exists, showing the card to a police officer or a cab driver will make your return easier.

➤ Do your best not to get lost. Not knowing where you are in a strange land can put you in an extremely vulnerable position. Make mental notes of landmarks as you leave your hotel. If you have a poor memory jot notes down on a notepad or trace your route on a compact city map that is small enough so that it does not draw attention to your being an out-of-towner. You should always endeavor to feel secure in your ability to retrace your steps.

➤ If you do become disoriented regarding your whereabouts, check with a shopkeeper or a police officer for directions—not a stranger on the street—unless you want to take advantage of being lost to get into a conversation

> I keep my stuff with me, even when I go into the bathroom.
>
> ♦
>
> *Joan Wallner,*
> *recreation coordinator*

and a relationship with the stranger. Even if you *are* lost, don't *look* lost. Carry yourself as if you know what you are doing and where you are going.

➤ When you enter a country, find out if you need an exit visa or if there is an exit tax for departure and if it must be paid in local currency. If there is an exit tax, set aside the amount you'll need right at the start of your trip. If you are unprepared for these requirements, the delay obtaining them can cause you to miss a connection.

➢ Earplugs can be a godsend to the traveler struggling with jet lag, especially if you are a light sleeper, or staying in a place where there are barking dogs, construction, or thin walls.

When I arrive at a new place, I always look around once quickly to check out the scene. I look for things that seem wrong or out of place, for people who make me uneasy. Then I trust my intuition — and move on if I'm not comfortable.

◆

Lorna Hanhy, artist

Chapter Three

MONEY AND SCAMS

We landed here in March. I wait tables
to make money. I can do this and
sail all around the world.

—*Waitress in a South Seas restaurant (1998)*

———

ew things are more crucial for a woman's safety and security on the road than money and access to money. It is much more difficult to operate independently if you are burdened by doubts about the reliability of your cash flow. Not too long ago, this was much more of a problem than it is these days. Travelers' checks were the only viable alternative to carrying cash and getting money wired from home was an expensive and complicated procedure.

Today it is a rare and isolated outpost that is without an ATM. Most major U.S. banks are connected with overseas partners through cooperative networks such as Cirrus, the Star System, and Global Access (yours are listed on the reverse side of your ATM card). Your local bank can check to make sure your ATM card will deliver cash in the country you are visiting, and what the foreign bank will levy for a service charge.

However, the technology can fail you. As credit cards rub against each other in your wallet, the magnetic strip on the back becomes worn and eventually will not trigger a valid response from ATMs. Foreign banks will *not* authorize a manual cash withdrawal for you even if you have your ATM card and offer to disclose your password. A card that won't work in the machine is worthless for providing you with needed cash *unless* it is a dual system card that can be used as either a debit card or a Visa or MasterCard credit card. Foreign banks will accept such dual cards and provide you with a cash advance based on the credit information on the face of the card.

If your ATM card is not also a credit card, ask your bank to issue you one of the dual cards. If they refuse because your credit history is inadequate for their restrictions, make sure you travel with a regular Visa or MasterCard, or some other credit card that you are sure will enable you to charge a cash advance. Remember that these cash advances carry enormous interest rates unless you pay them back during the first billing cycle. Although such cash advance transactions can be costly, they can be lifesavers.

> I basically don't carry cash. I get travelers' checks and use credit cards. I don't take any valuables, anything that I'd really miss if it got stolen.
>
> ◆
>
> *Saundra Haluska,*
> *dental assistant*

In rural areas or developing countries where ATMs may be a rare find, exchange some cash as soon as you arrive at the border or the airport to keep you solvent until you find the banks with the best rates.

When you travel to poor countries or regions, you should be aware that in the eyes of most of the natives, you are a very rich person, even if you spent your last dime setting up your trip. For many, the very possession of a U.S. passport marks you as wealthy—you come from the promised land as seen around the world in movies and American TV shows. When you are traveling in more developed countries, it is just as important to remember that your profile as a tourist or foreigner can mark you as an appealing target for scam artists and thieves.

Most Americans have not grown up in a thriving street market culture, and many novice travelers have a difficult time bargaining or understanding the psychological, emotional, and cultural currents at work with foreign merchants. If, on the other hand, you think of yourself as a savvy haggler or bargainer, it is wise to recall Rudyard Kipling's famous line: "Here lies a fool who tried to hustle the East." Chances are, the good deal you think you got also left a big smile on the merchant's face, an ideal circumstance. Enjoy the challenge of haggling in street markets, but don't expect to outsmart the locals. Try to find out if there are any special rules of the game you should be aware of, especially what actions on your part might signify serious interest you might prefer to keep to yourself.

Con artists and sexual predators can be a problem both at home and in foreign countries. The main difference lies in your heightened vulnerability when you are abroad. You may be hesitant to offend, feeling that you are misjudging cultural differences or language nuances, and therefore be hesitant to rebuff people even when your personal warning bells are ringing. Remember, the dangerous con artist can move quickly from someone who is merely trying to part you from your belongings to someone who may seriously harm you.

There are techniques to help you turn up the volume on your inner warning bells. The best defense is to have a roadmap of some of the more obvious tactics predators worldwide use. Gavin de Becker notes seven tactics in his book *The Gift of Fear* that apply not only to sexual predators, but also to con artists of all types in all cultures. (This book is must reading for all women travelers.) You may have experienced most of them at one time or another, but it can help to assign them names to help alert you. De Becker's seven tactics are: Forced Teaming,

Charm and Niceness, Too Many Details, Typecasting, Loan Sharking, The Unsolicited Promise, and Discounting the Word "No." These are simply stratagems that can help a predator to invade your personal space, create unsolicited links, maneuver you with charm, distract you with too many irrelevant details, manipulate you, create indebtedness where none exists, and basically help an intruder refuse to take no for an answer.

All scams, sexual and otherwise, attempt to shift control from you to the con artist. A recognition of these tactics can make an enormous difference in how you choose to respond. For example, Forced Teaming attempts to create a phony link with you. Let's say you're claiming your baggage in an airport and a man who has overheard your conversation comes up to you and says, "I can tell from your accent that you're from Minnesota, so am I! We Minnesotans need to stick together, let me help you with your bags." This might be a perfectly innocent offer of help from a nice man, but it may just as easily be an attempt to create a familiarity that does not in fact exist, in order to get you to let your guard down long enough for him to steal your bags or hustle you for sexual favors, or both. Be wary of people who take advantage of information gleaned from things you wear (like clothing with a logo or message) and your luggage. Watch out for people who use your first name too often or too soon.

In short, pay attention to any warning signal that intuition or common sense tells you is inappropriate.

$\mathcal{T}ips$

➤ Guard your PIN carefully, whether it be your ATM PIN or your telephone credit card number. Stand close when you punch it in at a pay phone. Phone card thieves work public places with binoculars. Peter's PIN was spotted by a thief at Kennedy Airport who ran up hundreds of dollars in calls to Ireland. If this happens to you, the phone company will clear the charges off your bill if you can make a good case that they break your normal calling pattern.

➤ Check the expiration dates so that your credit cards (and your passport!) do not expire while you are traveling. Make sure you get your own card back when you hand it to a clerk. Check with your credit card companies about what additional services they offer, such as travel insurance and guarantees for merchandise.

➤ It's easy to feel safe and comfortable on a plane, but if you leave your seat and you're traveling alone, take your bag with your onward tickets, money, and passport with you. You may feel secure enough leaving your things with a seatmate you've been talking with for hours and with whom you have established some rapport. Let your intuition guide you, of course.

In Bangkok, it's fun to ride *tuk-tuks*, the little motorized rickshaws you see buzzing around all over the place. But be careful, sometimes the drivers are in cahoots with merchants such as tailors and jewelers. So instead of getting to your destination, first you are pressured to visit an establishment or showroom on the way. Refuse, make a stink.

◆

Margaret Bradford,
photographer

I put my cash in my pocket, instead of in a wallet. I basically strip my purse, I have one charge card, that's it. So if my purse gets stolen, I'm not financially crippled.

◆

Chris Minner,
wife and mother

➤ Know the currency. Take along a pocket-sized calculator to figure the various exchange rates you encounter. If you're moving from place to place and rate to rate, the conversion can become confusing and a mistake can cost you plenty.

Consider making a chart that you can glance at so that you can get an immediate idea of what something costs in U.S. dollars. Do not allow a shop-keeper to pressure you into a fast transaction. The foreign currency values initially might be confusing and you can lose a lot of money if you don't take the time and effort to know what things are really costing.

➤ Stash your U.S. money and your foreign money in two different places in your purse so that when you reach for the local money no one sees a stack of valuable and attractive U.S. bills. The separation also makes it easier for you to differentiate between the values of the two currencies. Keep small amounts of money for incidental purchases separate from your main supply so that you do not need to expose your billfold when you're buying small items.

> Cabbies are often the first scam artists you have to deal with on arrival. The basic scam is taking the long route to anywhere. So it might be wise to take a little map with you and figure out where you're supposed to go. Cabbies also offer to help you find a hotel and if there's some sort of kickback involved, it might not be the best choice of hotel for you. They know you're brand new in the country. They're picking up virgins at the airport.
>
> ◆
>
> *Fay Faron,*
> *private detective*

➤ Whenever possible change your money by withdrawing it from an ATM. You'll get a better rate than with travelers' checks or cash, and it's convenient. Watch your back at the machine, just as you would at home. But remember that each withdrawal carries a service charge. Most international airports and train stations are equipped with ATMs. Change enough on arrival to get you through the first night. You don't need the anxiety of looking for an ATM in addition to the stress and excitement of arrival in a new locale.

➤ If you can afford it, keep at least a hundred dollars of American cash with you for emergencies. U.S. money is still one of the most popular currencies in the world and if you run out of the local currency, you'll be able to handle emergencies even if the exchange rate is unfavorable for you. Carry fifty or twenty dollar bills. Since the U.S. hundred dollar bill was redesigned, it no longer is as universally appreciated and accepted as it once was. In addition, keep a few one and five dollar bills with you, especially in developing countries. They make appreciated tips.

> My main key is keeping things as close to my body as possible. I carry a very tiny purse that can hold only a wallet and an aspirin case. I can wear it under my coat and I can wear it inside a dress. I bring it around to the front of me. If I am going to carry my wallet in a pocket, I make sure it is a deep pocket in front of me.
>
> ◆
>
> *Lynn Hassan, artist*

➤ No matter how tempting it may be, avoid the black currency market. Saving a few dollars (or even more) by changing money illegally is not worth the risk for at least two important reasons. One is that you could end up in a dangerous foreign prison for years. (Read Peter's book *Nightmare Abroad* if you want a picture of how grim this can be!) Another is that you could be swindled by a cheating money changer. In many of the countries where a black market deal would be alluring, the currency is unstable and frequently devalued. That often means bank notes with high numbers are retired out of circulation, replaced with newly designed bills that have fewer zeros. Unscrupulous money changers sell unsuspecting travelers old—and worthless—currency that looks just like the real thing, because it once was. Sometimes it's counterfeit. Some even sell the much less valuable currency of an adjoining country to tourists who cannot read the local languages and only look at the numbers on the bills.

➤ When you go out, always carry enough cash for at least one direction of bus or cab fare and enough to make a phone call. It is also wise to carry a pre-paid phone card.

➤ Take your sweet time counting your change from cab drivers, whether you're in Paris or Phnom Penh. You're at the mercy of cab drivers when you're flustered by language, holding up traffic, and the driver has added on all sorts of special charges beyond what's on the meter. Some of the worst offenders are in Paris and Rome; among the best and most honest are those in London.

➤ Keep track of what you charge to your room so that

In Jamaica, I got to the airport and the taxi driver came up in a very aggressive manner, and even after all my traveling, I was still naive I suppose because I got in his cab. He took me all over Kingston, through the neighborhoods, and ran up quite a bill. I'm very careful now to check with the official dispatchers in the airport.

◆

Karen Sandel,
international consultant

you can check it against your bill. Mistakes are made. Perhaps the hotel staff may be arrogant regarding requests to amend your bill. In that case, be polite and persistent. Don't hesitate to ask for the manager.

➢ If you are traveling far from the world's major capital cities, consider the value of an American Express card. American Express now offers credit cards that do not carry an annual fee. These cards will provide you with access to American Express offices worldwide, where you can receive forwarded mail. If you run out of funds, transfers to American Express offices are simple to conduct.

I don't put my wallet or anything of real value in a day pack. I keep my keys in a pocket that's on my body, not in an outer jacket pocket. I want them in my skirt or in my pants and I make sure my pocket is deep enough so that they won't fall out when I sit down. One of the things my sister has done is to sew big, deep additional pockets in pants.

◆

Lynn Hassan, artist

Chapter Four

DRIVING

The street was very much thronged, and I thought the crowd a more
civil and orderly one, than an English crowd. The men did not jostle
or push one another, or tread upon one's feet, or kick down one's
shoe heels, or crush one's bonnet into one's face, or turn it around
on one's head, all of which I have seen done in London streets.

—*Fanny Kemble,* Journal (1835)

Women can look like particularly easy targets to carjackers and smash-and-run thugs. Even with a man
in the car. Peter's mother was traveling in Italy with
his sister and her husband (and their children) when she
refused to become a victim.

Vesuvius was in back of them, the blue Mediterranean to
the left. Of course the car doors of the Volvo were locked. The
windows were up, too. They were on the main waterside road
going north towards Naples, still not quite in the city itself, just
in an ugly industrial sprawl. They stopped at a red light.

Peter's mother was in the front seat; his brother-in-law was
driving. Suddenly a guy on a motor scooter pulled up to his
mother's window, and smashed it with a huge drill bit (his
sister kept it for a souvenir). Glass shattered everywhere,
including all over his mother.

Then the robber put what Peter's sister describes as "his big
fat hairy muscley arm" through the space where the window
had been and grabbed her purse. He didn't know Peter's
mother. She held on to it and held on tightly. His brother-in-

law started hitting the invading arm from the driver's side and Peter's sister screamed loudly and relentlessly.

After what seemed like a couple of minutes to them in the car, the potential robber pulled his arm out as the light changed and they drove to a fancy hotel where, as his sister remembers, "Everyone apologized in the name of all Italy and the Pope, and gave us coffee."

They filed a police report, but of course the thief was never found, and the window was repaired.

Despite the happy ending, in retrospect Peter's sister has second thoughts about their actions. "Tell your readers that we did the wrong thing," she says. "If we had thought first then we would have stepped hard on the gas immediately."

You may not wish to run a red light into oncoming traffic, but it might be a better alternative than standing still at the mercy of an assailant.

Of course, to do what Peter's sister was suggesting, you have to know whether you can, in self-defense, cause serious bodily harm to another.

A study commissioned by the Automobile Association in England found that up to 70 percent of women worry about their personal security and safety when they are behind the wheel. Among the tactics used by women in an attempt to reduce their odds of encountering trouble, according to the AA researchers: avoiding unfamiliar roads and roads they fear will be deserted—especially at night, and dressing like men while driving alone.

Tips

➤ Most experts agree the safest thing to do when faced with a purse snatcher is to let go and leave. If you keep a photocopy of your passport in a separate place from your purse, the closest American consulate can replace it for you in a few hours.

➢ Lock the car doors whenever you leave the car, no matter how safe the situation looks. With the power locks that most rental cars come equipped with, you can lock the doors without drawing attention to your action. It is always more difficult to get someone out of your car once they're in than to keep them out to begin with.

➢ For the same reason, lock the doors when you are in the car and while you're driving. This way, you're in a better position to decide who gets in the car with you. Unfortunately, carjackings occur and women can look like vulnerable victims. Simply keeping the car door locked can prevent the casual car jacker and thief from getting into your car.

A woman I know was rescued by a cab driver. She was being hassled on the street and he escorted her into his taxi. But the guy who was hassling her came after her inside the car. The cab driver screamed at him and gunned the car in his direction. Later my friend wondered if he really would have run the other guy down. I guess you never know about something like that until it happens.

◆

Anonymous

I lock the doors when I'm driving and I'm aware of my surroundings. I'm not paranoid, but I check to make sure no one is following me. I don't drive with my windows down, even in the summertime, because of carjacking. At night I park close to where I'm going, and always in a lighted place.

◆

Lorna Hanhy, artist

➤ Gas up when the tank is half empty to avoid running out of gas or to keep from being forced to look for gas in neighborhoods you might otherwise avoid, especially as a woman alone. In some countries, 24-hour gas stations are unknown. Try to fill up the tank before you go to sleep at night so that if you need to put miles between you and whatever or whomever you want to get away from during the night or in the morning, you need not worry about fuel.

➤ Much of the world drives on the left-hand side of the road: the British, their former colonies from India and Hong Kong to Australia and New Zealand, along with Japan and Ireland. If you are going to rent a car and drive on the left, do not expect to just jump in the car and take off on a marathon ride the first day. It takes at least a few days or more of extra-careful driving to get used to the opposite side of the street and to looking right first at intersections, instead of left.

If I feel another driver (my experience has been that truck drivers are among the biggest offenders) is gaping at me, or worse, making lewd gestures, I begin picking my nose—really digging—and this seems to turn them off.

◆

Laura Spooner, mother of eight

Renting a car with an automatic transmission will make the transition easier, although cars equipped with an automatic may well cost more to rent.

➤ The same cautionary note goes for being a pedestrian in these places.

➤ If you are traveling with children, whether they are toddlers or teens, be especially careful to show them—and remind them daily—how the traffic moves differently. It is all too easy to forget, with potentially disastrous results.

➤ If you are shipping your own car to a left-side driving country, or taking a British-style right-hand drive car to the Continent or other places where the driving is on the right side of the road, expect even more trouble. It is extraordinarily disorienting to be on a strange side of the road and drive from the wrong side of the car. Distances are difficult to judge, passing on a two-lane road is excruciating—you must get your car into the oncoming traffic lane before you can see if any traffic is headed at you. Allow at least two days to get used to that phenomenon before you take off on a long drive.

I rented a car from Hertz in Japan, planning to drive from Hokkaido through the country-side to the northernmost village of Japan, Wakkanai. As I left the airport, I realized I simply could not read any of the road signs. I immediately was getting lost, stymied by my inability to read Japanese. I returned the car to Hertz and took the train to Wakkanai.

◆

Anonymous

➤ Lower your tourist profile at gas and food stops by keeping guidebooks and maps hidden under a local newspaper. There is no need to advertise that you're just passing through. A paper book cover can be made out of a local newspaper (the type we used on high school textbooks) for guidebooks. Camouflaging the guidebook is an easy device to help set the ground rules for interaction with the locals. They don't need to know as soon as they set eyes on you that you're a tourist. But don't be furtive when you look at your guidebook and risk attracting unwanted attention with your self-consciousness.

➢ Check rental cars for signs that identify them as rentals. Since a rash of tourist shootings in Miami, the state of Florida no longer uses special—and easily identifiable—license plates for rented cars. Some car rental companies still adorn their cars with bumper stickers to advertise their services. Pull them off. You do not need to yell, "I'm not from around here!" as you drive through strange neighborhoods.

➢ There are thousands of high-way crimes in the United States. Rest stops at night are particularly dangerous for single women. A cellular phone that is both visible and within easy reach is a good crime deterrent.

Once on the Autoroute in France, driving from Brussels to Paris, I filled the gas tank with the cheapest fuel at the station. I should have read the sign on the tank and checked my phrase book because I filled the car with diesel. After a few miles, the car started sputtering and barely made it to the next gas station where they drained the diesel and filled it with regular.

♦

Anonymous

➢ Carjackers often operate in pairs. They are often armed and approach from both sides of the car when you are parked or stopped. Your best chance of survival (assuming you can't escape with the car) is to hand over the car immediately, and run.

➢ Don't be coerced by clerks at the rent-a-car counters who try to sell you insurance. If you rent with a gold-faced Visa or MasterCard, you may well be covered completely. Before you go, check with both your credit card companies and your car insurance carrier to determine if you need the extra (and usually very expensive) insurance offered by the car rental companies. This is a lucrative trade for them and the clerks can be quite pushy about signing you up for extra and unnecessary expensive insurance.

➤ For those who do not want to appear to be driving alone, a company called The Safety Zone offers a bizarre but potentially useful product called the Safe-T-Man. This is the catalogue description: "Designed as a visual deterrent, Safe-T-Man is a life-size, simulated male that appears to be 180 pounds and 6 feet tall to give others the impression that you're protected by a male guardian while driving in your car." Safe-T-Man has a moveable plastic head, wears a black baseball cap and sunglasses, and can be deflated for easy portability. You can dress him to suit the weather and occasion. Safe-T-Man costs $120, a carrying case and pump is extra. Of course there is a toll free number for this quiet companion: (800) 362-5500.

➤ If someone is hanging around your parked car

I keep my pocketbook and any other attractive looking possessions on the floor or under the passenger seat. Thieves are always looking for a quick and accessible grab. Sun roofs, for example, can provide easy entry to your car at a stop light.

◆

Brenda Davis, family manager

If I'm driving, I take my dog with me and if the motel allows dogs, then I stay there and if not, I just keep driving. I try to avoid people when I travel. I go cross-country a lot. I have my routes planned so all my friends know what route I'm taking and who to call if I break down.

◆

Kat Gonzales,
911 dispatcher

when you return to it, walk past it as you assess the situation. If you have any doubts, summon help. Do not give the benefit of the doubt to a potential robber or assailant.

➤ Park close to well-lit exits in closed and underground garages.

➤ Avoid road rage by steering clear of the behaviorally impaired on the highways. Keep your profile low on the road with simple courtesies: save your horn for emergencies, use the passing lane only for passing not for cruising, don't sprawl across two parking places, use your high beams only when they won't distract other drivers, and don't tailgate other cars.

I drive to Kansas all the time by myself. I always make sure I have enough gas to get me through to the next place that's well-lit. I never stop at the roadside rests because there are so many transient people there. If I have to stop and sleep, I stop at truck stops. And I always make sure my doors are locked.

◆

Connie Bennett, businesswoman

Chapter Five

DEALING WITH
OFFICIALS

They think it rude to laugh, but they never hesitate to yawn.

—*Lady Anne Wilson,* Letters from India *(1911)*

———

The light changes on the Berlin street and as the traffic starts to move I feel my VW camper bumped and scraped by the flat bed trailer truck in the lane next to me. After it hits me, it keeps going, around the Golden Angel circle in the Tiergarten. I honk my horn, chasing after the truck.

I'm thinking hard about what I'll say when I do catch up with it. I've just moved to Germany and at this point speak very little German. The truck keeps moving and I lean on the horn, chasing the truck. The driver is obviously trying to ignore me and just drive away. I keep after him and finally he stops.

I get out of my bus and with my limited vocabulary say something along the lines of, "You beat my auto." But he knows what happened. The trailer created a huge scratch and dent in my VW. What he says back to me I cannot understand.

"We'll wait for the police," I say. I wait and wait. I'm not about to leave the scene to call them because I assume he'll just drive away again. Finally a police car shows up, but it's not a traffic cop.

"Bitte, Konnen Sie ein umfall Polizei anrufen?" I ask, pleased with myself that I'm able to request the accident investigation

cops. The truck driver and I stand, he next to his rig, I beside my VW, in a misting rain. The traffic police arrive within minutes and invite us into their wagon, to sit around a table and fill out the accident report. The truck driver avoids my eyes.

Herr truck driver talks first, in German. I take deep breaths and pick up a few words. "The woman was doing something wrong. And then she...." I cannot understand what he says next. Again he says, "And then she..." And again I cannot understand what he's charging me with doing. He goes on and on as the police study his piles of official paperwork.

Finally I interrupt. "*Bitte*, please. May I say something?"

The truck driver is dismissed. He smiles at the police and thanks them. The procedure seems so unfair to me, but I insist on trying to tell my side of the story. Using my driver's license, a pack of cigarettes, and my passport for models, I demonstrate the accident on their table with a few words of German and a crash noise. They look at my documents and tell me I can go home.

"But what happens now? Do we go to court, to a judge?" I ask.

At last, the younger cop speaks to me in English, "Don't worry, he was wrong. His company must pay. But you shouldn't have passed him."

There is no point in pushing the issue even though I hadn't passed him. I am jubilant.

As we American women travel, we must always remember that even in societies such as Germany that seem on the surface so much like our own, customs and laws can be radically different. It is usually worth the time and effort to at least obtain a cursory understanding of the laws in the countries in which you intend to travel. The American guarantee of innocence unless proven guilty is absent in most of the rest of the world, including Germany.

Many of the destinations for tourist and business travelers are directly influenced by the Napoleonic Code, the laws drafted for France by Napoleon in 1804. These statutes spread to conquered territories and were instrumental in the development of laws in much of the rest of the world. The direct result is that Americans detained in most foreign police jurisdictions are presumed guilty unless and until innocence is proven.

Avoiding confrontations with authority figures is an important goal.

Tips

➤ If you have an accident, prepare yourself to encounter male police. Try to stay as calm as you can. Stand your ground if you know you're right. Be patient and expect to be on the receiving end of male chauvinism. If you are politely persistent, and allow unimportant (under the circumstances) references to your sex to pass without much challenge, you may well be able to transcend such age-old obstacles.

➤ Expect, in some developing countries, that some rogue policemen may offer to drop serious charges against you for sexual favors. Take your chances with their criminal justice system—refuse politely but firmly—and face the charges.

➤ Cash bribes are part of routine business with

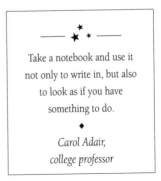

Take a notebook and use it not only to write in, but also to look as if you have something to do.

♦

Carol Adair,
college professor

authorities in some countries. Knowing when and how to offer to settle differences with police requires querying local residents and relying on your own intuition. Using phrases such as, "Is there a way for me to pay this fine now so that neither of us are delayed by a trip to the police station…" or "How much is the fine and can I pay it now…" allow you to offer cash directly to a policeman without calling it a bribe. When you are dealing with more than one cop, such an opening is riskier because one may fear the other will report him for taking the cash.

➤ Try to manipulate where you pull over if a police car signals you to stop. Seek a locale with plenty of light and action such as a busy street corner or a gas station.

➤ If you wish to carry a firearm, it is wise to make sure you are familiar with applicable gun laws. You can reduce the possibility of trouble with the authorities by keeping any weapon in a holster. In many jurisdictions a holstered weapon is not considered concealed

> In Italy, I've been told that if you're stopped by a policeman and you smell a rat, ask to see his ID. Thieves have been known to show a fake plastic police badge.
>
> ◆
>
> *Stefania Payne, marathoner*

and can be stashed legally under an automobile seat. The offices of state attorneys general and foreign consulates can provide you with details of their gun control laws.

➤ Similarly, if you plan on carrying Mace or any kind of pepper spray or any other protective device, know not only how to use it, but know the law—foreign or domestic— that applies to it. Mace and pepper spray are illegal in many countries. If you do take them, pack them in your checked bags.

➢ Before you go through the metal detectors at airports and wherever else you may encounter them, remove any bulky metal jewelry and other metal that may make the alarm go off. Passing quickly through the metal detector not only expedites your progress, it also keeps you from being forced into a secondary search with an official who may—for some reason—get more curious about you and your business in his or her country. Delays also allow thieves to make off with your belongings which have emerged from the x-ray machine.

➢ If you are carrying a Swiss Army knife or other tool, don't keep them in your purse during air travel, consider checking them. They show up in a security check of your carry-on baggage and may get confiscated or just impede your journey. Do not carry on things that can be interpreted as illegal or threatening.

> Customs agents in China made me take all the batteries out of my things and put them through security for me. I was supposed to be able to pick them up on the other side, but they were all mixed up and I ended up with six. I kept saying, I only need two, but they didn't understand. I also had trouble there because I had film wrapped in lead to protect it from the x-rays. Even after they understood what it was, they insisted on going through absolutely everything.
>
> ◆
>
> *Jan Fleming,*
> *AIDS educator*

➢ Do not agree to transport or deliver anything for anyone you've met on the road.

➢ Many foreign transit systems work on what purports to be

an honor system. You buy a ticket, or a pass valid for several trips or good for a period of time, and are not required to show it to anyone in order to board the bus or train. However, periodically inspectors check for valid tickets. If you are unaware of the system or how it works and are caught without a ticket or with an expired ticket, apologize and make it clear that you are a confused foreigner. Often the guards will let you off with a warning, especially if you can convince them that you will buy a new ticket immediately. If you fail, you will be faced with a sizable fine.

When you're traveling by rail in France, make sure to punch your ticket at one of the orange pylons by the door to the tracks. If you forget to, and you run into a conductor having a bad day, play the dumb foreigner.

◆

Margaret Bradford,
photographer

➤ Take a moment to assess any order from an authority figure. Remember that some will be using their badge of office to try to take advantage of you and will consider you especially vulnerable because you are a foreigner and a woman. Try to be as matter of fact as possible and give yourself an air of importance that puts you on an equal footing.

The biggest problem with customs was coming back from Thailand and going into the Seoul airport. I got pulled out of the line and completely searched for drugs. They said that the Bangkok police had tipped them off that a woman with blond hair was carrying drugs. I was really nervous, but I had to give them all my bags and let them search me.

◆

Kirsten Wivel, student

➢ If you are arrested, demand an opportunity to be put in direct contact with American consular officials. Don't be surprised if your demand is delayed or if the Americans do not respond immediately. Request to be housed alone or with other women while in custody. Do not allow police badges to be overly intimidating. If you do not trust the policeman questioning you, ask to see his superior. Don't beg or plead. Act businesslike. Your second priority after informing the American government of your predicament is to alert a friend in the U.S., someone you know who will work tirelessly and efficiently to get you home.

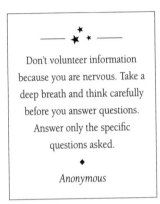

Don't volunteer information because you are nervous. Take a deep breath and think carefully before you answer questions. Answer only the specific questions asked.

♦

Anonymous

➢ If you are jailed abroad, one valuable tactic can be to publicize your plight widely in the U.S. media. The best technique to accomplish such publicity is to rely on a trusted friend back home. If you worry you may be arrested overseas, it's best to set up arrangements for help from Stateside contacts before you leave.

➢ Never threaten foreign authorities unless you are sure of your power and are ready to risk losing the battle.

➢ If you have a dispute with a hotel or a shopkeeper that is impossible to resolve and you feel you are being intimidated, consider telling them you will call the police. Most merchants who are in the wrong, or are deliberately trying to cheat you, will not want local authorities involved and will back off from the conflict if you are about to introduce the police.

➤ Your appearance can instigate unnecessary interaction with authorities. Dress and act conservatively. In some countries it is illegal, or at least frowned upon, to wear army surplus clothing if you are a foreign civilian.

➤ Guidebooks offer valuable information, but do not consider them guaranteed authority. The best of them will candidly admit that they go out of date quickly. Make sure you become your own authority by double check-ing crucial information such as changing laws, new government policies, and restricted locales. All U.S. Passport Agency offices provide updated travel advi-sories, as do U.S. embassies and consulates. The Bureau of Consular Affairs also offers advisories over an automated fax system that is available 24 hours a day at (800) 647-3000, via the mail from the Office of Overseas Citizen Services, Room 4800, Department of State, Washington, D.C. 20520, or at their website at http://travel.state.gov

Coming out of Russia when it was still Communist, officials looked through everything. They wanted to know why I had a book called *Hospital*—it was about Bellevue Hospital in New York. What can you do but stand there and answer the questions as briefly as possible?

◆

Annette Leyden, retired medical librarian

➤ When conditions are particularly dangerous, as long as you don't mind the government knowing where you are tramp-ing, it is worthwhile keeping the closest American consul informed about your wanderings. If you disappear, they may help organize a search. U.S. consular help varies widely country to country, official to official, ranging from lifesaving to anemic and useless.

➤ Try to obtain general letters of introduction from officials or business figures of the countries you are visiting. Sometimes these can be used to help you out of tight spots.

The worst experience I had was traveling from Turkey back to America a few years ago. We always bring food back from Turkey because most of the stuff you can't get in America. The food we were bringing back was legal. We marked it on the customs forms. But just because we marked that we had any type of food with us, the officials went through our clothes, even our underwear, everything. They even opened all the food just to make sure that nothing illegal was being snuck in. When we were putting my clothes and the food back in the suitcase they didn't bother to provide any other containers (because they opened the cans and they obviously had juices in them) so they spilled all over. My clothes and everything were almost ruined. We complained but nothing happened.

♦

Defne Ezgi, student

Chapter Six

LODGING

The houses are in the water, and look dirty and uncomfortable
on the outside; the innumerable quantity of gondolas, too, that
look like swimming coffins, added to the dismal scene. Venice
on my arrival struck me with horror rather than pleasure.

—*Lady Elizabeth Craven*, A Journey through
the Crimea to Constantinople (1789)

———

*G*uidebooks can be quite wrong. Always second guess your
guidebook with your feelings and on-the-spot information you get from other travelers or trustworthy locals.

In a pouring rainstorm in Wellington, New Zealand—
guidebook and map in hand—I find my way up and down the
hilly San Francisco-like streets to an old Victorian guesthouse.
The guidebook suggests a congenial atmosphere, rooms with
private baths, and a bargain price. From the outside, the place
looks rundown, so even though I had made a reservation, I
decide to inspect the room.

I ring the bell and tell the fellow my name. He leads me
through a dingy hall and down into a half basement where he
opens a door.

"Here's the room," he smiles, "and the ladies is over there."
He points to the communal toilet facilities. The room smells
terrible, looks worse: dirty, with a late-Goodwill decor.

"The guidebook says the rooms come with bathrooms."

He frowns and says, "We're a budget hotel. No private baths."

I ask the price.

"Eighty-nine dollars, plus GST." GST is the ubiquitous New Zealand Goods and Services Tax, a substantial hit added to everything that would bring this dingy room in at over a hundred dollars. That would be ten more than quoted over the phone and more than the guidebook predicted. Besides, the place is unacceptable.

"Thanks," I say, "I'll talk to my partner about it."

He scowls at me. "There are other places down the street. Look for a place called the Thomas Cook. That should suit you," he says sarcastically.

As we look for the Thomas Cook, we see signs on some elegantly refurbished Victorians offering daily, weekly, and monthly accommodations. We hail a woman walking out of one of them.

"Hello. Do you work here? We need a place for the night."

She stands in the rain in her windbreaker and red sneakers, telling us that she does indeed work for the outfit and is walking down to the reservations office. She starts to explain complicated directions to the office.

"Do you want a ride? Get in out of the rain," I suggest.

> I was going to Mexico City alone, but there was a tour on the flight so I asked the host of the party to recommend a hotel. He did so and even let me ride along from the airport to the hotel with the rest of them.
>
> ◆
>
> *Mary Alvarado, holistic health practitioner*

We drive up to the main hotel and office, and the place looks well over our budget.

"These nice people," she says to the desk clerk, "gave me a ride out of the rain and need a room for the night. Maybe there is one right here so no one needs to go back out into the rain."

The clerk's fingers click on the keys of the computer terminal while I suggest the hotel might be too pricey for us. The clicking continues and we stand there together without any more words, we three women.

"How about an apartment for a hundred dollars including taxes?"

"Great," I say, "I'll take it. Thanks to both of you."

Two bedrooms, two bathrooms. Elegant. A washer and a dryer for our road-dirty clothes.

As I sit in the living room, I look through the guidebook. I discover the Thomas Cook is one of the most expensive hotels in Wellington. I feel like calling the guy back at the dump up the street and describing my bargain suite at half the price of the Thomas Cook. Instead, I walk over to my kitchen and take a cold beer out of the refrigerator.

Tips

➤ Register in hotels with your last name and first initial. Do not advertise your gender with your first name or a Miss, Mrs., or Ms. title.

➤ Using the stairs can isolate you in a lonely stairwell. Take the elevator, but make sure you're happy to go up or down with whomever is already in the elevator.

➤ Don't leave your room key (with the identifying hotel

Whenever I go to a city where I've never been before and haven't had much contact, I find out from a guidebook or travel agent what the best hotel is and I stay there. It's mostly for safety reasons—that way I know I can avoid bad neighborhoods.

♦

Michelle Oltman, wine importer/exporter

name and room number) on a bar while you're drinking or on your restaurant table while you're eating. You don't need to help a con man find you later, or come on to you with a line that includes information (your hotel name and room number) that confuses you because you don't understand how he got that private information.

➤ If you fear someone is following you, don't go to your room. Go to the front desk and ask for an escort to your room. Usually that will intimidate the follower. If you're still concerned, tell the hotel employee and return with him or her to the front desk before you arrive at your room, so the predator won't learn your room number.

➤ If you're using a laptop computer to keep in touch with the homefront, be aware that some hotel telephone systems won't respond to your modem because of complications caused by the switchboard system or by digital phone equipment. Most hotels these days use a direct line to connect with credit card

My friend Kitty and I decided to take a motel room advertised for twenty-five dollars. She was trying to open the door when a bunch of guys came out of rooms on either side of ours. They were all around Kitty—not nice—saying, "Hey, you need some help opening your door?" We finally got in the room. We could hear through the walls; they were listening to us through the vents. I was scared, but Kitty was shaking. We left. The woman gave us our money back. We made a decision then: no rooms under fifty dollars, ever.

◆

Sophie Lemarie, accountant

companies to obtain authorization for charges. If your room phone balks at making an e-mail connection, ask the desk clerk to let you plug directly into the credit card line and simply dial the log-on number directly.

➤ Some hotels offer computer users a special jack, but if you unplug the telephone to hook up your computer to check your e-mail, remember that means the telephone can't ring. You might think if you're traveling alone and no one knows where you're spending the night that it doesn't matter if the phone can't ring. That's wrong. If there is a fire or other emergency in the hotel, the hotel staff may well use the phone to warn you.

➤ There are almost as many different telephone connector jack sizes as there are countries in the world. The American standard is the RJ-11, but without an adapter for the system used by the country in which you're traveling, it will be difficult to access your computer network. Either take along adapters (available from travel and electronic equipment stores)

I usually call before I move into a hotel to find out how the neighborhood is. I often ask the manager or people who live there. If I need to park in a parking complex or lot, I try to park as close as I can to the hotel. A lot of places have security people who will escort you to the car.

◆

Erica Noffsinger, nurse

or use an acoustic coupler, a device that fits onto the phone's mouthpiece and earpiece instead of directly into the phone line. One company that stocks just about all possible adapters is Austin House, available at (800) 268-5157.

➤ Making a personal connection with the desk clerk and concierge can be a life saver. They are instant access into the local culture and, especially if they are women, easily accessible to friendly overtures. Just let them know you are a hotel guest and that you want to know the local customs. You'll find most clerks and concierge staff eager to share suggestions, favorite sites and restaurants, and survival tips. You may even make a friend.

> Don't spread your clothes and toiletries and books so completely throughout the room that a rapid exit will be difficult. Each evening, repack most of your things even if you're planning on spending the next night in the same room. That way, if something goes wrong and you decide to leave quickly and ahead of schedule, you won't be slowed down by looking around the room for your journal or a stray shoe.

> Consider using the hotel safe for valuables, but better yet, leave that jewelry you need to worry about at home and travel with just what you can comfortably keep with you. If the maid steals some cloth-ing or a few books, it won't be that big of a deal. By using the hotel safe, you're alerting the staff that you've got some-thing of consequence to stash, and while in transit you

---

I make sure that the hotel I stay in has a gym. I keep hydrated before, during, and after plane travel. For me, these two prac-tices are essential for staying healthy on the road.

◆

Diana Wilson, chief financial officer

I never get a room by the elevators. I make sure that the hotel has an electronic security pass on the door. I don't stay in hotels with doors that open to the outside.

◆

Aggie MacLean, business consultant

might not want to trust the hotel staff without getting to know them.

➤ Fire truck ladders generally don't extend beyond a building's seventh story. Consider insisting on rooms between the second and seventh story. Ground floor rooms are more vulnerable to casual break-ins than rooms above street level.

➤ Leaving the TV or the radio on when you're out of your room makes it appear as if the room is occupied and may discourage thieves. The "Do Not Disturb" sign can trigger the same response.

➤ A compact and portable electric sound alarm is available that you can quickly install on your hotel door and take with you when you check out. The noise is so piercing that all but the most determined crooks will run from the pain it causes. News reporters used these effectively in Somalia. Noise alarms are also available that are triggered by compressed air; these can be used against bothersome dogs.

➤ All but the best hotels may lack adequate smoke alarms. You can buy a portable battery-powered smoke alarm at most hardware stores to take with you.

➤ If you are excessively concerned about fire and smoke, you may want to consider packing a product called the

> I was on the train to Salzburg last year and I happened to hear somebody speaking English. I asked him for his advice because he looked okay and he told me about a really great hostel. Sizing up strangers is all by the seat of my pants, but so far it's been all right.
>
> ◆
>
> *Donna Louie, scientist*

EVAC-U8 Smoke Hood. This is basically a plastic bag that fits over your head and is attached to a filter that cleans carbon monoxide and other toxic fumes out of your air supply for twenty minutes. The cost: about $70 U.S., available from Traveler's Selections (800-362-5500), travel specialty stores and catalogues. Bring it on airplane flights too; those who survive air crashes are often overcome by toxic fumes.

➤ If you don't trust hotel door locks, you may want to bring one of your own. The Magellan travel catalogue offers a universal supplemental lock for about $12 U.S. that can be fitted onto most doors and dresser drawers. Magellan is available at (800) 962-4943 or at their Web site: www.magellans.com. They also offer an ingenious little wedge equipped with a suction cup that can be used to block sliding glass doors.

➤ A cheap low-tech security device is a garden variety rubber doorstop you buy at a hardware store. Bring two and jam them under your door if a hotel's doors and locks seem insecure.

➤ Hotels in some countries demand that you leave your passport with the front desk overnight, either as collateral

I almost always have a reservation and always get a confirmation number. A flight confirmation number is essential, especially if you have to switch flights.

◆

Tara Lynch,
public relations

or while you are being registered with the police. Wandering a strange place without the security of your passport may be an unnerving experience and there is a trick to avoid such a predicament. The U.S. government will issue you a second passport if you can convince a consular officer or a passport office that you have a need to travel to a place where a stamp in your regular passport will cause you future problems. For example, an Israel stamp will make travel to most Arab and many Moslem countries difficult for you. Once you get that second passport, leave it with hotel clerks and keep your main passport with you.

> House exchanging is a great way to get inside a country. Not only do you usually get to live in a lovely dwelling, you may well get the use of a car along with the house, and neighbors who are excited to meet you and help you figure out what's going on. There's also a good chance they will invite you over for dinner, so you'll get inside somebody else's house, too. We have had wonderful luck doing house exchanges.

♦

Amy Valens, teacher

➤ Many hotels charge absurd fees in addition to local telephone company charges for calls back home, and those local telephone companies usually charge much more than American fees. If you plan to call home, get a wallet-sized card from AT&T or Sprint or any of the other phone companies that lists, country by country, local numbers to call to get connected with an English-speaking operator Stateside. Then you can charge the call to your telephone company credit card or your home number.

➤ Instead of an expensive phone call, consider sending faxes. A detailed letter gets home for a fraction of the cost of an average telephone conversation. Include your hotel number so that your friends and family can call you back. Calls from the States are almost always dramatically cheaper than calls back to the U.S.

I feel very comfortable looking for housing at train stations in Europe. I don't always go to the unofficial tour guides, but I look at what the atmosphere is like and in many situations I feel comfortable going to one of the people who meets the trains. Generally I choose one who has a name tag that identifies him and can also show me a book of pictures of the places that he's representing. I know there are many people who don't feel comfortable with that, who worry that they may get taken down some dark alley. But I feel like I can identify those who are legitimate, if not officially sanctioned. I've had wonderful experiences in Rome and Amsterdam doing that.

♦

—*Amy Valens, teacher*

Chapter Seven

CHOOSING ITINERARIES
AND COMPANIONS

The difference between landscape and landscape is small,
but there is a great difference between the beholders.

—*Ralph Waldo Emerson*, Essays: Nature *(1844)*

━━━

I rarely consider hiring a guide. But there are exceptions, and I often just find guides without asking. I've gone fishing after midnight at the edge of a campground in France with local women I met while brushing my teeth. We had few words in common, yet the feeling was so good. I don't even fish, but I held a pole, watched them and their menfolk demonstrate what I should do to catch a fish—until my feet froze. Those women were my impromptu guides.

Once in Mexico, a little boy followed the car after recognizing the California license plates. He ran alongside us, yelling.

"Missus! Let me take you—not much money—to the artists' houses. Not much money! Please!" He was barefoot, running faster.

My cynical traveling partner dismissed the boy, saying he was probably just a hustler.

But something about the look of boy intrigued me. "Let's stop the car and ask how much."

The price was so little, we followed him against my companion's wishes.

The boy took us to the home of a family that makes papiér-maché mirror frames, frames for pictures that are painted in garish colors, and other tourist trinkets. The man asked us about our work, and to show him an example of it.

"We're jewelers," I said, showing him the gold ring I was wearing with an opal set in it that I had made.

We shared stories with the craftspeople; they learned about our life and work, we experienced a behind-the-scenes look at the gross discrepancy between a Californian and Mexican artist's lifestyle. Our ad hoc guide made that possible.

In Australia, I asked for a restaurant recommendation while buying a bottle of wine at a store. The clerk pointed to a man next to me who introduced himself as a local restaurant owner. He smiled and said, "Please come to my restaurant. I used to be the chef at the best restaurant here."

I asked him what he served and he said it was just a fish and chips joint, "But I promise everything is fresh. Follow me!"

So we followed him to the little shop and he told us he'd stay open late for us, as late as nine-thirty.

We showed up at nine and he led us to the back of the restaurant, out into the warm night, to a small table. By the time our custom-prepared food arrived—it was delicious—we were chatting with his wife, his two young daughters, and two friends who stopped by—both members of the local activist Aboriginal community. One of them fetched his *digeridoo* from his car and offered Peter and our son Michael lessons.

Once I had a fellow traveler who stuck to me like glue. I had a one-and-a-half-hour layover, so after twenty minutes of this person not leaving me alone, I said, "Excuse me, I have to go to the restroom." When I came back, I made sure to sit between two other people.

◆

Laurie Hobbs,
computer technician

We were invited to their cultural center the next day for a personal guided tour, sans tourists, of the museum and bush.

In the museum I decided it best to keep my irritation to myself as I was told, and reminded by signs, that the *digeridoo* should not be played—or even touched—by women. It is their culture.

These, of course, were lucky breaks with happy endings. Often it is valuable to make use of established formal tour services.

Current information is another useful guide. Keep in touch with the local news, not only to know what events may be occurring that you might want to attend but also to keep up to date regarding changing political situations and weather that could influence you to change your itinerary.

Choosing traveling companions depends on individual proclivities. Some of us enjoy the dynamic of hanging out with groups. For those types, organized group excursions provide an opportunity to meet other like-minded travelers. The possibilities for such encounters are enormous, from the low-budget and somewhat communal bus tours run by the Green Tortoise company, to the political trips to various hot spots like the California-Mexican border organized by activists such as San Francisco-based Global Exchange, to the various classes abroad offered by many university extension programs.

> I feel comfortable traveling with women. Sometimes I travel with a group if it's only women, just until I get my bearings in a country. In India I was with a group for the first ten days and by then I was comfortable with what was going on, I could see how people operated and I knew what the problems were. Then I was ready to take off and go on my own.
>
> ◆
>
> *Barbara Grosso,*
> *teacher*

If you prefer just a single companion, it's probably a good idea to choose a friend you know well so that you'll enjoy common likes and dislikes, schedules and idiosyncrasies. Remember, the one thing you can't do without in a travel companion is a good sense of humor.

Tips

➤ If you do want to pay for professional tours, pick guides carefully. Get recommendations from the hotel's concierge or front desk. Otherwise consider talking with independent taxi drivers. Start by taking a short trip. Ask lots of questions, and if you feel comfortable, make a daily deal. You'll get a car and driver, a guide, and a potential protector.

➤ When you arrive in a new city, take a quick tour to familiarize yourself with what's where and what's available and what you may wish to avoid—by bus, tram, or boat. Often the public transport system provides a very inexpensive and comprehensive route around town.

When I was in Greece, I was with a friend and we were out with a couple of guys we'd met when we landed. They had a pickup truck and my friend was riding in the back; at one point I turned around and they were gone. I totally panicked and I had the guy who was driving take me back to my room. I asked around about these two men because some of the other women at the hotel knew them and swore up and down that they were okay. She came back several hours later fine, but the experience really startled me and reaffirmed the need to communicate, know where you and your companion are going.

◆

Lisa Woldin,
research administrator

➤ Keep in touch with important news developments that affect changing travel risks. For example, a careful traveler planning a trip from Australia to England just before the 1991 Gulf War would have kept track of the increasing tension on the Iraq-Kuwait border and checked with the airline to make sure a Sydney to London flight was not refueling in Kuwait City. Sometimes travelers don't think to check where their flight across the world is scheduled to stop along the way; a troublesome stopover in some countries could be particularly problematic for women.

➤ The *International Herald Tribune* and *USA Today* are not available everywhere. Pack a small, high-quality shortwave radio so that you can keep in touch with the news from the BBC World Service (much more comprehensive than the Voice of America).

> I'm extra careful if I happen to be in any European town or city where there's a large sports event going on. What they call "soccer hooligans," often English guys, can be totally dangerous when they're on a drunken rampage.
>
> ◆
>
> *Stefania Payne, marathoner*

➤ Even if you don't want to lug a laptop computer around the world with you (or can't afford the investment in one), you can stay in touch with the news back home via e-mail and the Internet. Most cities of any consequential size these days offer cybercafés, or other public places such as airports, with computer terminals where you can log onto the Internet for a small fee, send and receive messages, and check for the latest news from home.

➤ As soon as you choose a spot for a stay even as short as an overnight, make yourself known to shopkeepers and restaurant operators in the immediate vicinity of your accommodations. They'll help you pick the best places to eat and sights to see, but they may also quickly come to consider you one of their own and warn you of trouble or call for help if you appear to be in danger.

➤ If you stay abroad for a while and get a job or enroll in school, consider varying your route to work or class. The sight of a foreign-looking woman, traveling regularly along the same streets, can stir the interest of predators. You will also find new neighborhoods to explore.

➤ If you travel by intercity bus and must stash your luggage in the underneath storage compartment, choose the compartment on the curb side of the bus and then make sure you sit on that side of the bus. When the bus makes stops, you can watch from the window to make sure your bags are not intentionally, or mistakenly, unloaded in the middle of nowhere, never to be seen by you again.

Two of my trips, one to Europe and one to South America, were with the same person. We sort of complemented each other. She was good with some things and I was good at others. It wasn't anything we agreed on, it just happened.

♦

Barbara Grosso, teacher

➤ If you are visiting a place where political demonstrations, labor strikes, and other mass gatherings are occurring, check with locals and the media so you can avoid them if you wish. You may wish to watch (or even join) these events, but just as is the case at home, they can be dangerous. Mob hysteria or police actions can make a benign crowd deadly in a hurry.

➤ Festivals can be not only fun, but also a wonderful window into another culture. Some events in some places do not offer a welcoming atmosphere for women. When in doubt, it's a good idea to check with local women about the customs at play.

➤ Gypsy taxis cruising for fares can pose a serious threat to women travelers, especially in poor cultures where robbing one traveler can be more lucrative than driving a cab for a year. Mexico City is particularly notorious for crimes against cab passengers. Use taxi stands at airports, major hotels, and bus stations for the safest rides.

➤ When traveling with children or teens, make clear plans for what to do in case you are separated, where to meet, whom children should be told to approach. If the children are small, dress them in bright clothes that will be easy to spot. Consider giving them a security whistle to wear around their neck, as long as they are mature enough not to blow it unless it is necessary. Children should be able to remember the name of the hotel they are staying in; if they are not, give them a business card from the hotel to carry in their pocket.

➤ When you ask questions across cultural and linguistic barriers, make sure you are simple and clear when you speak and avoid questions that require only a yes or no response. Phrase your query with constructions such as: How do I get to…? and Where is this train going…?

When I was younger, it was too hard to be two middle-aged women traveling alone. They put us at the worst tables in restaurants, sometimes there were plenty of parking places at hotels and motels, but we were told there were no rooms. So I began to join groups to China, India, Australia, all over the world, and things were taken care of for us ahead of time. Of course there were people embarrassing to be with who were rude or loud, but accommodations almost made up for that. For ten years I traveled with a woman with whom I had nothing in common. Sometimes I'd come home and say "never again," we were so different, but I realized that's what got us through difficult situations. What upset her didn't bother me at all, but when I was bothered, she wasn't upset. It worked out beautifully.

◆

Christine Shordike, retired

Chapter Eight

HEALTH

Scorpions haunt all the houses. Their bite is poisonous.
The effects are more or less violent in different constitutions.
Some persons will remain for eight days in convulsions,
foaming at the mouth, and the stomach swelled; others,
by immediate remedies, do not suffer much.

—*Madame Calderón de la Barca*, Life in Mexico (1843)

———

*A*s my mother-in-law never fails to remind me, "If
you've got your health, you've got everything." Health
concerns are crucial during the preparations for your
trip, even if you rarely fall ill.

Health insurance for the road is worth the investment. Just
ask Michelle Annand. I encountered her sad story in the *Otago
Daily Times* while traveling through New Zealand on my way to
Milford Sound. I read it with some peace of mind as I had
checked with my insurance carrier before I left the States and I
knew I was covered in New Zealand (or anywhere in the
world). I just needed to pay up front for any covered medical
attention and then get reimbursed once I returned home.

But Ms. Annand set off for six months in India without
insurance. All she wanted was inspiration for her work as a
painter and a chance to study classical Indian dance. For a
month all went well. Then she broke her leg.

"It happened by sleeping in a yogic position and getting
quickly out of bed," she told the *Times*. She took a step "with a
leg that lost circulation and it twisted under me," and then was

forced to endure a two-and-a-half hour taxi ride to the hospital. "I held my leg together with pillows while the taxi bumped around on monsoon-damaged roads."

For six days she languished in the hospital, her leg in a cast but not set properly and not healing. The basic necessities were a battle with an unsympathetic staff: water, bedding, toilet paper. Finally she managed to get a phone call through to her parents who arranged for a trip home and traditional Western medical care.

Michelle Annand's advice to anyone who listens is simple and direct: "Don't go to a Third World country without insurance. Breaking a leg may not be a disaster in many places, but in India it definitely is."

Tips

➢ Even if you risk living without insurance in the USA, invest in insurance for the duration of your trip. You will be surprised at how relatively cheap short-term health insurance can be. You do not want to be at the mercy of questionable doctors speaking in languages you do not understand in hospitals with substandard sanitation.

If I'm going on a trip for more than 3 or 4 days, I take my gym clothes and make sure the hotel has facilities.

◆

Susan Bucher, advertising account executive

➢ Look for an insurance policy that will pay to transport you to Western-class health facilities.

➢ Kidnap and ransom insurance is available if you fear you may be snatched during your trip. Because the odds of such an occurrence are remote, some brokers offer as much as a million dollars worth of insurance for a premium as low as $500. Some policies offer advice from security professionals for avoiding kidnapping, trained negotiators if a kidnapping takes place, and a vacation somewhere safe once the rescue is made.

➤ Check to make sure your prescriptions are properly filled. Peter went to the trouble of getting an Imodium script (back before the anti-diarrhea drug was available over the counter) in case he got sick on a trip to the Afghan-Pakistan border. He got sick and took the pills. He got sicker and called me at home in California. I told him to read the codes on the tablets. The pharmacist had mistakenly filled the bottle with the arthritis drug Indocin. One side effect of Indocin is diarrhea.

I ran out of my medication in Portugal. I went to a pharmacy and showed the pharmacist the bottle, asking if he could refill the prescription. He did so on the spot. What a relief. I got the pills without having to go to a doctor who may or may not have spoken English. A friend of mine told me he did the same thing in Bolivia without even having a labeled bottle to show. He just asked for the medication at a drug store.

◆

Anonymous

➤ If you are a gourmand, be cautious in southern Europe about purchasing farm or home-preserved produce, such as mushrooms preserved in olive oil. Improperly canned food can contain botulism.

➤ Especially when traveling alone, consider checking in regularly with a friend or partner back home. If you're sick and miss a call, you'll know someone will become concerned. If you miss two, your contact should try to reach you. And if you stay out of touch too long, you should have a deal with your friend to initiate a thorough search. If the cost of long distance check-in calls is an inhibiting factor, come up with a simple code: call collect using a name that your contact knows simply means you are okay.

➢ In regions where health concerns are serious, check in with the American consulate. If there is no American consulate nearby, friendly nations often share in-country information with American travelers. Try the British, Canadians, Australians, and other well-traveled English speakers first.

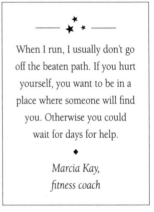

When I run, I usually don't go off the beaten path. If you hurt yourself, you want to be in a place where someone will find you. Otherwise you could wait for days for help.

♦

Marcia Kay,
fitness coach

➢ Call the International Association for Medical Assistance to Travelers (716-754-4883) for a list of English-speaking doctors worldwide. They can also be reached by e-mail: iamat@sentex.net or visit their website at: http://www.sentex.net/~iamat

➢ Know some of the warning signs that you may have picked up a parasite: diarrhea, constipation, unusual flatulence, joint and muscle aches, anemia, allergies, skin conditions you can't figure out, sleep disorder, teeth grinding, chronic fatigue.

➢ Your period may come unexpectedly and you ought to be

equipped with enough tampons and pads to last through at least one entire period. You'll be surprised at how many foreign shops are closed on Sundays and holidays with which we're unfamiliar. Even international airports might be of no help. At one important Western airport where I landed there was an apologetic note posted explaining that the tampon and pad vending machines were permanently shut down because of vandalism.

➤ Healthy pregnant travelers should be over the worst of any morning sickness by the fourth month, and full of energy at least until the sixth. Check with your doctor or midwife before any strenuous travel, of course, and don't push yourself too hard. Allow for plenty of nap times. Consider avoiding those regions of the world where health care does not meet the standards you enjoy at home. When you establish your itinerary, you may also wish to avoid those regions that would require you to take the kind of preventive medications that you would not like your baby to be subjected to through your body.

➤ If you're pregnant, stay away from traveling to exceptionally high altitudes except in pressurized aircraft. Check with your doctor about what times during your pregnancy are least risky. It is safe to say that cruises should be

Many travelers to developing countries get diarrhea shortly after they arrive, it just goes with the territory, and you'd best be prepared for it. Bring toilet paper, handi-wipes, aloe vera gel to relieve soreness, plus whatever medicines your doctor and your witch doctor recommend.

◆

Janis Blaise, homemaker

avoided during the final trimester—you don't want to be stranded at sea and in labor.

➤ Even healthy and fit women find that pregnancy can change their walking and running abilities. Keep to well-lighted streets with plenty of people around if you're strolling alone.

➤ If you discover that you're pregnant while traveling in remote places away from well-trained doctors and the latest medical equipment and medicines, take your vitamins and consider coming home to take advantage of modern health care facilities.

➤ On long flights across time zones and the international dateline, keep track of your biological time if you take birth control pills.

➤ I travel with an enormous stash of vitamins and food supplements collected in a compartmentalized plastic case with labels identifying each vitamin. Although it is important to consider the potential vulnerability of traveling with pills carried outside of their original containers, I am not worried about my vitamin supply. My theory is that any suspicious customs agent

—— ✦ ✦ ✦ ——

Before I get into any new water, I read it. It's hard to tell what lies beneath the placid surface. Are there old pier pilings, sunken ships, rocks? Are there strong rip tides or strange currents? One of the best ways to decipher what lies below the surface is to ask the local people. It's also a great way to meet someone new and sometimes a way to begin a friendship. Swimmers, boaters, lifeguards, harbor masters, and fishermen tend to be pretty friendly people and all of them can give you an idea what the lake or river or ocean is like.

◆

Lynne Cox, endurance swimmer and writer

will be convinced that they are vitamins both because I'm not hiding them and because of their rank smell. Of course, trips along established drug-smuggling corridors require extra sensitivity to this issue. My suggestion is that all women take along at least high-potency vitamin C, a B complex, digestive enzymes, and melatonin. Although there are some skeptics, I am convinced melatonin helps ease jet lag.

➤ For over-the-counter remedies, I suggest all women take along at least a hefty supply of both aspirin and a non-aspirin pain relief compound (if you travel with your pre-pubescent children, they should not take aspirin because of the danger of Reye's Syndrome), antacid tablets and an anti-diarrhea medication. In addition to whatever might come to ail you on the road, by bringing these medicines, you're in a position to help others you meet along the way.

➤ Other things that are so common in your medicine cabinet that you may not think to take along: Band-aids and rubbing alcohol. If your destination is even on the fringes of the First World, bring toilet paper. It is light to pack and as you use it, it leaves room in your luggage to bring back souvenirs. If you run out, even in the heart of the Third World, you can often obtain some emergency toilet paper from five-star hotels in capital cities. These hotels are also accommodating safe havens if you need to get off the street for a breather. If you act as if you belong, you can use the toilets, the telephones, browse the much-too-expensive gift shop, or just relax in a comfortable lobby chair—all for no charge.

➤ Coffee addicts should bring along Nodoze or Vivarin to fend off caffeine withdrawal headaches when traveling in areas where coffee is either hard to find or tastes so foul that it's difficult to swallow.

➢ Wash your hands repeatedly, and always before eating. Keep a stash of anti-bacterial moist towelettes (available at most drugstores) for cleaning up when the washrooms are dirtier than your hands. Keep your hands out of your mouth and eyes.

➢ Carry an extra pair of eye-glasses and a copy of your eyeglass prescription. Take along extra wetting and disinfecting solutions for contacts.

➢ Especially in hot climates, wear skirts or loose pants and cotton underpants to reduce the likelihood of vaginal infections.

Whenever I get into the water for the first time, I always slide my feet. That way if there are any stingrays on the sandy bottom they shuffle away, and if there is any glass or other debris, I may hit it with my big toe, but I won't step down and cut myself on it.

♦

Lynne Cox, endurance swimmer and writer

➢ I carry *feuilles de savon* no matter where I go. These are paper-thin leaves of soap packaged in a folder the size of a credit card and available in boutiques that specialize in skin care products. After I wash my hands, and before rinsing them, I wash the tap itself before turning it off. If there aren't paper towels available, I just shake the water off my hands.

➢ If London is a transit stop for your onward journey, an excellent resource is the chain of British Airways Travel Clinics. There are 40 of the clinics throughout the United Kingdom, including sites at Heathrow and Gatwick airports.

They are open to all travelers, not only BA customers, and offer advice on health conditions in most countries of the world. The clinics provide vaccines and no appointments are needed. Clinic locations are listed on the BA Web site at www.british-airways.com/bans/lworld/clinic.htm

I was about 23 and with my family on a two-day cruise down the Nile on a luxury boat when I became very sick from the food. As I was lying in the hotel room later, a guy came in to change the towels and said something in broken English to the effect that he knew how to make me better. I thought that he had some inside knowledge about people who get sick over there. He told me to roll over and in my weakened condition, I did. I felt really vulnerable and then he started rubbing my back. At that moment my stepfather walked in, looked at the situation and told this guy that it was time to leave.

◆

Stephanie Secrest, photographer

Chapter Nine

ATTITUDE

The Poles seem a lively people. The women of the lower class wear
upon their heads a wrapper of white linen, under which their
hair is braided and hangs down in two plaits. I observed several
of them with a long piece of white linen hanging round the side of
their faces, and covering their bodies below the knees: this singular
kind of veil makes them look as if they were doing penance.

—*William Coxe,* Travels into Poland, Russia, and Sweden *(1792)*

————

*T*he attitude with which you approach a situation on
the road may be misperceived by others. When Poland
was behind the Iron Curtain, there were strict rules for
tourists. In order to get most visas, you had to pay in advance
for an unseen hotel room of the government's choice. "The best
hotel in Sopot," was promised us by the government-run Orbis
tourist office, and the fading turn-of-the-century Grand Hotel
probably was the best. There was no choice, the other hotels
were off-limits to American tourists.

Swans swim directly in back of the Grand on the Baltic Sea.
In the room, a colorful china platter is cemented to the wall to
replace broken bathroom tiles. Holes are drilled through the
platter to accommodate the bath tub spigot and the hot and
cold water controls. On the inside of the door, a list is dis-
played in a plastic frame. The awkward translation states the
house rules. The first is that no women who are not guests in
the hotel may come up to the room. Another makes it clear that
additional blankets cost extra.

We wander with our son Michael around the resort town and stop in a bakery to buy some bread. Peter orders. The woman behind the counter looks at me, not him, and makes it clear in terse Polish that I ought to be performing the duties of a wife. And that includes choosing and ordering the family bread. I remember only a few words of Polish, but her meaning and body language is clear. The same act is repeated in a cheese store. I am berated by the clerk who can't understand why Peter is ordering, clearly I look Polish and he doesn't.

We eat dinner in the hotel. The dining room is high ceilinged, with dilapidated elegance, the waiter dressed in frayed and formal black and white. We decide to risk still another fish from the grossly polluted waters of the East Bloc and eat a delicious meal of trout, potatoes, and cabbage salad, all washed down with a nice bottle of wine.

Peter and Michael head up to the room for the night and I order coffee and an after-dinner drink, pulling out my notebook to write. When I next look up, the waiter is sitting alone, all the other diners are gone. We say goodnight and I leave to return to the room.

Three steps up the grand staircase that curves up behind the reception desk, I hear the desk clerk speaking loudly in Polish. I keep climbing. She is obviously angry at someone. I look back again and realize that the woman's angry words clearly are designed for me. Using

---
★ ★ ★

I bought cheap clothes in India. I wore what the natives wore. If they wore scarves, I wore scarves. If everyone wore long skirts, I put on long skirts. It saved me from a lot of hassle. People who would normally bother tourists wouldn't bother me because it looked like I was living there and it made me more comfortable.

♦

Barbara Grosso,
teacher

hand gestures, she points that I should come down the stairs. I do, curious about her problem. With another furious burst of words, she points me to the door.

"Pardon me," I say in precise English, "but I don't understand what the problem is here." I pull out my room key.

"Your passport, please," she says. All clerks in the tourist hotels speak English.

"You have it. Laufer, Sheila Swan."

She apologizes. I don't bother to tell her my mother's maiden name was Soja and her mother's Kozloski. But clearly my Polish ancestry is apparent in my looks, and because of my chic Western clothing, I stood out among my distant Polish cousins. Obviously the woman initially thought she was preventing a Polish call girl from violating hotel rules.

My somewhat disdainful attitude allowed me to take control of the moment.

Rather than becoming angry in such situations, my attitude is to be calm and firm.

Tips

➢ Walk and act with a sense of confidence and purpose. Few things attract hustlers more than an obvious tourist standing around looking at a loss for what to do next.

I like to visit places during their worst weather: Tucson in the summer, Alaska in the winter, Asia in monsoon season. Different things happen, you get people in hotels and restaurants who are grateful for your business, you meet locals who are pleased or bemused that you would visit in bad weather. But be sharp, because the thermometer of the unexpected gets high. In Calcutta for instance, be careful crossing a flooded street—you might fall in an open manhole and drown.

♦

Margaret Bradford,
photographer

➣ Don't generalize; learn the specific subtleties of the region where you're traveling. Islamic culture, for example, differs greatly from one country to another. You can't go wrong in any Moslem country by dressing modestly in loose-fitting clothing that covers your arms and legs. But even though mosques in Turkey, for example, are available for visits by non-Moslems, they are off limits in Bangladesh for those who are not members of the faith.

➣ In the stricter Moslem countries, where alcoholic drinks are available only in the first-class hotels catering to Westerners, drinking in the hotel bar and restaurant alone is considered inappropriate behavior for women by local standards.

➣ When applying for visas to strict Moslem countries, improve your chances of being approved by wearing a hair-covering scarf for your visa photographs, and bringing a male companion with you if you meet with immigration officials in person.

I live in New York, so I'm always watching my back on the street. A couple of times I think I dodged getting mugged by actually turning around when somebody was too close to me. I turned around and looked at them.

When I come in the building, I make sure there is no one behind me. Once I'm sure I was in one of those schemes where someone tries to distract you and somebody else tries to pick your pocket. I just turned around and looked these people in the face. It was in a Post Office vestibule. One person was not going out the door and I think other people behind me were going to come and take my purse or take something out of my purse. I shoved this person out of the way and went out the door.

◆

Ann Rosen, writer

- Keep track of yourself and your belongings, especially in tourist-filled public places where one crook working in concert with another can distract you while the other lifts your valuables. Typical distractions are spilling something on your clothes or shoes, appearing to be in distress and needing help from you, jostling you and drawing your attention with apologies.

> I always bring reading material so I don't have to talk to anybody I don't want to.
>
> ♦
>
> *Celeste Comi,*
> *sales and marketing*

- You are not welcome everywhere, and in some cases there will be no specific rules, regulations, or signs instructing you to keep out. You must see and sense the exclusion. For example, most *kafenia*, the cafés in Greece, are culturally off limits for women. A woman alone can expect to be made to feel quite uncomfortable in *kafenia* and in cafés throughout the Balkans.

> I think people who haven't had negative experiences tend to be more relaxed and not worry about safety. I think that because I've always lived and traveled in places that are considered safe, I haven't had to watch out for my safety. I just *assume* that I'm safe.
>
> ♦
>
> *Salli Miller,*
> *businesswoman*

- Dress down, but not sloppy or too revealing. Fancy clothing draws hustlers who figure the expensive attire must mean there is more of value available with a little effort.

- If you travel with a laptop computer, chain it to something that doesn't move if you leave it in your hotel room. A port in most laptops will connect with a lock available at computer stores.

➤ To help deal with offensive toilet facilities, pack paper toilet seat covers with you. They're available at most Stateside drugstores. Another product to consider is called Le Funelle. It is a paper funnel that makes it relatively easy and neat for women to urinate while standing into a toilet. Made of paper, Le Funelle comes in packs of four and 20 and can be ordered from Magellan's "Essentials for the Traveler" catalog, available at (800) 962-4943.

➤ In toilet stalls, keep your purse on your lap. If you use the hook on the door, a thief can grab it from over the door and run while you're stuck in the stall.

I put light around myself. And I make sure that my AAA card is paid up to date so that I've got the long distance towing. Those are my two biggies for travel in the States.

In the Amazon once, we got up the first morning and there was the uniformed guy with the gun, and the jungle beyond, and the old rickety planes. Were we frightened? Well, there really wasn't anything to do. When you're in the United States there are so many presumptions: that you can pick up a phone and call for help if something goes wrong. But out in the middle of the Amazon River it's obvious that most of the people don't live in the cocoon of safety we live in. It was one of the most important things about the trip, to just let go of trying to be in control.

◆

Rose Anne De Cristoforo, writer

Chapter Ten

FINDING YOUR SCENE

In traveling we visit names as well as places.

—*William Hazlitt,* Notes of a Journey
through France and Italy (1826)

———

A few months after the Velvet Revolution in Czechoslovakia, we arrange over the telephone to rent an apartment in Prague. The landlady tells us she'll meet us outside the building at an appointed hour. We drive up and down the street, not finding her or the place.

The weather is freezing and I walk into a bar and restaurant across the street from where I think the apartment must be located.

The bar is full of men. Working men in their work clothes, just off the job for the day, standing around with pitchers to fill with the bar's draft beer to take home after work. They drink beer in the bar before going home with the pitcher.

I stand in line. When it's my turn, I ask the man pumping beer if he speaks English. The answer is no.

The saloon is decorated with American cowboy saddles and guns. The barman wears a leather vest and a cowboy bandanna around his neck. I ask for a glass of beer and if he speaks German. No. Then he disappears.

From the back room a woman comes out. My age, smiling.

"Can I help you?" she asks in an English accent I can't recognize.

And help me she did!

Stania is visiting her sister for the first time since the Prague Spring fourteen years before, when she had escaped the Soviet invasion—leaving her home and family for a new life in Canada. Her sister and brother-in-law are the proprietors of the restaurant and bar.

She calls out to the men in the crowded bar with their beer pitchers, asking about the address of the apartment. The debate is loud and there is no consensus. Fed up, Stania takes me into the kitchen and calls the number of the landlady. She speaks fast in Czech and hangs up the phone.

"She will come here," Stania tells me and smiles. Pointing to the woman cooking hunks of meat in a vat of hot oil, she announces, "That's my sister Elishka."

"Hello, Elishka," I call out. "My name is Sheila." Elishka speaks no English, Stania tells me.

I stay in the kitchen, with the women, as Stania talks. The landlady shows up and Peter goes with her, across the street, to secure the apartment. I learn about Stania's adventurous life as a nurse in the outback of Canada, she translates Elishka's stories about the struggle to build up the restaurant business. About how they're short-staffed because her husband is home ill, and they can't afford to hire more help, or trust unknown workers.

The next night we return to eat and visit. The restaurant is jammed. After dinner, I go back to the kitchen and announce, "I'm a good cook, I can help."

"No, this is special Czech food," Stania says, chopping onions.

"I can chop onions." We work, talk, laugh, and manage to find the time to drink a few shots of vodka together that the customers bring to us.

Elishka admires my scarf. I take it off and give it to her.

"Oh no," Stania says, "that's terrible. Now she has to give you something." And so: an invitation to her home the next day. The next evening I return to the kitchen and wash dishes.

Elishka laughs at me and finds enough English to call me, "You crazy American." Stania translates the rest of her sister's words. "We may not have the fanciest restaurant in Prague, but we have the only American dishwasher."

I know I have found my scene. I've found people with whom I can relate, and a safe and comfortable homebase in a

In Costa Rica, I'd meet someone at dinner and they'd give me rides or invite me to their houses. It's an amazing place. I wouldn't have gone to their houses—American paranoia. I'd take rides, though. How did I decide it was okay? Instinct, I suppose.

♦

Eileen Anderson, marketing

Sometimes language problems are really not barriers, they actually enable you to learn more about people and their ways than you could by using words. I've also discovered that whenever I am traveling alone in a foreign country, it always helps to sit near families. They are used to dealing with children who have the vocabulary of a three-year-old and usually don't mind helping a foreigner who also has the vocabulary of a three-year-old.

♦

Lynne Cox, endurance swimmer and writer

foreign city. It not only offers me protection, but also an entry into the non-tourist daily life of the people who live there.

Tips

➢ Pick a café near your hotel and take your coffee or tea there every morning. Stop by again for an afternoon break each day. In a day or two, you will be recognized by the waiters and waitresses. You can begin to get to know them and learn from them about their locale. You will also feel some sense of belonging by creating a familiar hangout for yourself. If you need help after a few days, the fact that you are a familiar face to the café workers will make it more likely that they will believe your story and respond to any plea for assistance.

➢ Your regular café also gives you an opportunity to leisurely observe the local women. From watching

I usually keep a small subset of the most important things in a bag that I carry with me. I usually keep books and food and water, because what's supposed to be a four-hour bus ride could turn into an eight-hour bus ride. I keep my passport in a little bag inside my clothes and keep money between my insole and my boot. Whenever possible, I choose who to sit next to on the bus, like an older woman or a woman with a kid. When I stop to rest I keep my leg through my backpack strap

◆

Robin Plutchok, public information officer

I was visiting Hong Kong. We were delayed for two hours. There was another single woman traveling and we started talking. She said she had reservations and we ended up staying together. It worked out well.

◆

Donna Louie, scientist

them you can quickly learn what passes for appropriate behavior, from clothing to public interaction with men.

➤ Try to stay in one hotel for a few days at a time. You'll begin to make connections with people so that you'll develop a comfort zone for the city where you're staying.

➤ Consider taking some classes, either private or at a public university. Language lessons are a terrific opportunity to meet other women (and men) with common interests with whom you may feel safer than with people you just meet randomly on the street. These classmates could make ideal casual dinner partners or partners for testing the local dance and club scene. You may even make a good enough friend to share expenses and room together.

➤ Take your own interests and hobbies, be it weaving, bird-watching, or whatever, and find clubs or individuals who are engaged in the same activities. Such a connection can provide an introduction to homes and experiences in a safe environment.

Since I'm often working when I travel, the work I do provides me with an introduction to local colleagues and their scenes. In Switzerland I walked by a gallery and saw something which spoke deeply to me. We went inside and very unsuccessfully tried to communicate in German with the proprietor. A lady there spoke to us in English. She took us to a show of the artist and then took us to a bookstore and helped me find a book about him. I contacted the artist and we all had dinner at her house. She turned out to be a pianist, about 80, very warm and welcoming. We've been corresponding for years now. They've become like relatives and we enjoy a close and warm relationship.

◆

Susan L. Roth, children's book illustrator

Chapter Eleven

ENCOUNTERS WITH STRANGERS

Oh the earth was made for lovers.

—*Emily Dickinson (1850)*

———

*D*ating is safe when your family has known his family as long as you can remember. Or is it? The important difference with dating while traveling lies in the mores and customs of a foreign country. Or does it?

When Peter was covering the run-up to the Gulf War, he passed through Dubai and secured a copy of the advice booklet the U.S.S. *Wisconsin* printed up in an attempt to keep its sailors out of trouble during shore leave. It's written in the quaint style of a stereotypical sailor—and from a man's point of view—but the suggestions regarding casual sexual encounters (listed under the subtitle, "The Gals") are worth repeating—both for the amusing look behind the scenes of how our Navy operates, and for the reminder it contains. The following is copied verbatim from the pamphlet, typography, punctuation, and all:

> Dubai is a very international city, but there are a couple of things we need to keep in mind here. Women are not treated the same as they are in the states. Some women (but very few in Dubai) still wear veils. If a woman has a veil on, DON'T speak to her or try for a "peek" under the veil, that's VERY BAD.

Rumor has it that there are some "professional ladies" but Islamic law forbids this activity so watch out.

There are, by all accounts, a lot of very nice women in Dubai (some Arabic, British, Oriental, Pakistani, Indian, etc.) Basically, unless the woman is wearing a veil, it's okay to talk to her. So…there's no reason why you can't meet that "special lady." *If* you *DO* meet that "special" little lady, and you find yourselves developing mutual urges, take the necessary "latex" precautions. A moment taken to don your "STDPO" (Sexually Transmitted Disease Protective Overgarment—you get 10 seconds to don it) may keep you from having your day and life ruined.

Basically, the Navy's advice to sailors works fine for adventurous women travelers, too. Perhaps you're not on vacation to date and you're not interested in dating and you want to avoid circumstances that lead to dating. The same sorts of behavior that communicate to men at home that you're not available for dating will work for you in most cultures around the world.

This book is about safety and security. Romance is about trust and magic. The guidelines for romance are the same at home and abroad. But dating and one-night stands can well cross over into safety and security concerns. It is imperative that you make the effort to learn the basic cultural differences between home and the places you travel. Showing bare legs

In Greece, another woman traveler gave me good advice: Greek men are honorable: if you say no, they accept it. The tourists, she told me, are the ones you have to watch out for.

♦

Sigrid Akkermann,
medical student

83

can be like announcing you are available for casual sex in some societies, similar unintended messages can be sent by drinking in public or even meeting the eyes of a strange man with a smile.

Tips

➤ Feel secure with your intuition. If you think you can read people well, don't second-guess yourself too much.

➤ As an American woman abroad, you will almost always stand out as different—often more appealing than the locals—to the resident men. Of course, this can be a plus. But be prepared for attention based on your nationality. The cliche—blondes being attractive to men in those regions where fair hair and skin are rare—is real.

➤ Consider hiding provocative or sexy clothes under an overcoat if you want to avoid attention on your way to a party.

➤ If you are at a bar or drinking with anyone you do not know well keep an eye and a

Yeah, I've had affairs while traveling. When you're on vacation, it's as though you're on the other side of the Earth—you hardly speak the language, he doesn't speak much English, but sometimes it just happens. Fortunately for me it's always turned out okay.

◆

Katie Brown,
travel agent

If I walk into a cafe in Italy and the guy doesn't say, "I'll make an amazing cappuccino for the girl with the blue eyes," I'd consider looking in a mirror to see if something's wrong. But I never consider their pledges of undying love.

◆

Alisa Roth, journalist

hand on your glass. Rophynol (also known as the "date rape drug") and other colorless, odorless, and tasteless tranquilizers can be slipped into your drink by men who prefer their sex with partners who are barely conscious. Rophynol is now being manufactured with a dye so that it is not colorless but there are many other powerful drugs that are completely invisible in a drink. Don't think it can't happen to you! Some women have not even been aware that they were raped until they saw themselves later on videos confiscated by police. Do not accept glasses of punch at parties where you don't know the host well.

➤ If you expect sex during your travels, remember that, depending on your destination, condoms may not be easily available. Some countries may offer no condoms, others may be substandard for protection against sexually transmitted diseases. Condoms should be stored out of bright light and away from heat. Check the expiration dates on the packages and look for condoms that meet international standards and so are labeled with the code ISO 4074-1:1990.

> When my sister and I were traveling, she was always smiling and looking in people's eyes, so I played the sour one. This confused the men who thought that my sister was asking for men to follow us.
>
> ♦
>
> *Amber Morris, singer*

➤ If you wish to avoid causal come-ons from flirtatious fellow passengers on trains and buses, you'll find women-only seats in India and some of the other former British colonies, and in many Islamic countries.

➤ A relatively safe place to meet men is in group situations. These can be an opportunity to meet like-minded companions and observe them in the company of others. Consider scientific expeditions, church services, language classes, sports events, a workout gym, or museum tours.

➤ Insist on a first date in a public place, in order get to know your companion in a safe environment. Do not go off on a lonely hike in the woods or a long drive in the countryside until you feel comfortable with him.

➤ A good device to keep a new date from feeling that he can expect something from you is to insist on paying your own tab. Keep enough money with you to pay your share, but do not carry so much cash that you make yourself attractive as a potential robbery victim.

➤ Double dating is useful for insuring that you are not alone with someone new, while retaining a romantic atmosphere.

➤ Persistent unwanted advances usually will stop if you really ignore the person after once, and only once, saying no. The important part is not to respond. Do not be reluctant to reject anyone who seems threatening or pushy. The advantage when you're traveling is that you can get out of town.

When going to a Middle Eastern or Muslim country, it's sometimes safer to wear a veil, just across your hair. Also, don't look into men's eyes. Eye contact in the Middle East means that you're trying to seduce a man. Cast down your eyes.

♦

Fariba Nawa, news reporter

Chapter Twelve

WHEN A THREAT IS REAL

This is the paradise of thieves. I think the whole population
may be divided into two classes of them; those who adopt
force, and those who effect their purpose by fraud.

—*Eliza Jay, Original Letters from India (1817)*

———

*O*ften Americans blithely travel around the world with two dangerous misconceptions: that the protection of the U.S. judicial system follows them across our borders and that if they do encounter trouble with a foreign government the U.S. cavalry will come riding to the rescue. Neither is true.

Perhaps because American society has a reputation for such violence, Americans—and this is particularly problematic for women—are susceptible to a false impression that foreign lands are inherently safer than their own.

Researching a project about Americans in prison overseas led Peter to a decaying colonial-era prison in Karachi, Pakistan where he interviewed a hapless woman from New York who had been arrested for heroin possession. In the filthy and noisy group visiting cell, Peter shouted back and forth with her, through barred windows covered with wire mesh.

"It is no place for a woman to be, I'll tell you," she said about Karachi Central Prison, "especially for a foreigner. The grounds are terrible," she points out the dust and mud and garbage. "Most of the time it's covered with water, so you have to walk through puddles. The food they serve you is beans and rice every day. If you have money, you can buy your own food. If you don't have money, forget it, baby. You starve to death. Some of the food they serve you has worms in it. I mean, this is no place for an American. You get diarrhea from eating beans all the time. You get a runny stomach. You have nausea constantly. You're throwing up. You get fever. Because the rice they serve you here in prison isn't clean, you have to clean it yourself. It's half-cooked. You have to cook the rest of it yourself. It's terrible."

She complained about the inadequate medical attention and explained the special pressures she faced in a Pakistani prison as a woman, including being forced to wear traditional Islamic-style clothing. "If I go outside my gate I can't wear my jeans. They won't let me. Because all the men will start staring at me and touching and everything. If it wasn't for the fact that I have a husband, I would probably be raped by now."

She recounted a story of being molested on one of her trips between the courthouse and the prison. "I almost got raped in the Black Maria, the police van that takes you back and forth. I knocked the shit out of the guy, plain and simple. He went to grab me. He tried to rip my clothes. He tried to rape me in the Maria and I just knocked him out because I am an American. I don't take no shit, you know? I'm American. I live in New York City. So I know how to handle people like that."

> The more simply I travel, the safer I feel. Unencumbered, I am able to be more receptive to what is happening around me.
>
> ◆
>
> *Amy Valens, teacher*

But for all her bravado, and despite the nasty nature of her crime, hers was one rotten existence. "I try to think of nice things, but most of the time all you hear is the people who are sick here in pain. You really can't think much. Most of the time I sit and cry. I try to think of nice things. But then when you do think of nice things, you end up being miserable."

She was happy for the opportunity to offer other traveling American women advice. "If you come to Pakistan, for people who like to travel, it's nice. Don't get in the business of heroin, because you're going to get in jail. Just like me."

But don't think that just because you're not in the illegal narcotics business, you are safe from the clutches of foreign police and jails. A traffic wreck in Mexico, for example, can land the driver in jail for the duration of the accident investigation.

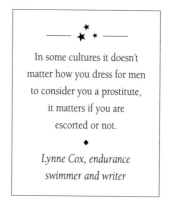

In some cultures it doesn't matter how you dress for men to consider you a prostitute, it matters if you are escorted or not.

Lynne Cox, endurance swimmer and writer

My friend JoAnne's car broke down in a questionable neighborhood in Spain. She was forced to leave the car parked on the street where it stopped while she waited several days for a special-order part to arrive. Fearing loss of or damage to the car, she bought handfuls of religious cards picturing the Virgin Mary and one of the baby Jesus. These she affixed carefully all over the car to protect it, crowning the hood with the picture of Jesus. When she returned with the spare part several days later, the car was intact.

Consider the customs of the country where you're traveling to cleverly avoid theft, threats, and damage.

In some places it's next to impossible to avoid the bad guys, unless you simply stay away from those places. Obviously dark alleys, threatening-looking neighborhoods, and empty streets are all the types of spots best left alone both at home and abroad.

But you might not suspect the Tokyo subway at rush hour as a haven for sexual predators. In an article for *The New York Times*, reporter Sheryl WuDunn interviewed one Samu Yamamoto, a middle-aged man who rode the Japanese subways grabbing at women—and who shared molestation tactics with colleagues. "When men and women are packed together, squeezed onto a train," he explained, "I think everybody has some kind of desire to touch someone else's body." Women passengers told reporter WuDunn stories of having their bras unhooked and being rubbed against by men, but being so tightly packed into the cars that they couldn't defend themselves or move away from their attackers.

My friend Lee Lapin is a safety and security professional, traveling the country running seminars and workshops about all manner of tactics and techniques. Lee's intriguing book *How to Get Anything on Anybody* is encyclopedic. We got together over crabs and clams at a beachside restaurant in California to discuss attitude as an element of safety and security for women travelers.

"What about turning on the tears," I asked Lee as we contemplated the desert menu. "If a woman could summon tears at will, is that a worthwhile protective device to try to stop an attack?"

The answer came without hesitation. "It's hard to do unless you're an actress and it's probably of very limited value. Somebody who really wants something doesn't care if you're crying or not."

Screaming definitely is in a different category for Lee. "Screaming often has a shock affect on the attacker and it's probably better to scream than not, in any case I can think of.

Screaming may or may not bring help, but it may buy you a second or two of time because the guy—let's assume it's a guy—doesn't expect it. That's one of the reasons martial artists use a loud cry, it kind of stuns the person for a second, gives you a split second to do something. And of course, it might bring help, if you happen to be in a place where people help screamers."

Lee studies martial arts, owns a wide variety of firearms and knows how to operate them—even shoots them on ranges for fun—and is emphatic about the importance of being familiar with weapons, if a traveler decides to take one on the road for protection. "It's wise to sit and review times when you were stressed or afraid to see what your reaction was. If you feel you want to protect yourself with something, look for mechanical things like whistles or mace,

I always wear running shoes, I never wear something I can't move fast in.

♦

Marilyn Byus,
planner

whatever would be allowed where you're traveling. Then get practice using it. Learn limitations. Learn both your limitations and the things that may help compensate for your limitations."

Some of Lee's specific advice includes learning that a weapon, pepper spray for example, is not a cure-all, that it does not stop some people who are extremely drunk or on some types of drugs. You need to be close enough so that the spray affects your attacker. You want to plan an escape route so the gas does not impair your ability to run away. "Spray it on a wall and stand next to the wall to get an idea of what it feels like," Lee suggested. The same sort of familiarity is crucial for any weapon you contemplate carrying, or picking up, such as a club or a stone.

We talked about appearance. Is a pretty woman more likely to attract attackers than a Plain Jane? Lee was less concerned about subjective beauty than appearance as it relates to why a predator may be interested in targeting a specific traveler.

"If you look like you might have money, if you look drunk or available for a casual pick-up, you're much more likely to get hit on." Lee's advice is specific: take off your jewelry, don't display things other people really want, don't wear pierced earrings that can get pulled out of your ear. But Lee rejects the idea that physical looks play a role in vulnerability. "I think the factor is more in your bearing, your walk, your attitude, the way you carry yourself, than what you actually look like."

Perpetually anticipating the worst would make for a depressing vacation, Lee pointed out, and used an old friend's experiences in Asia as an example of how standing out in the crowd is not necessarily to be avoided. "Her hair is bright red. She trekked through Nepal and got a kick out of everyone coming up to her and touching her hair. They'd never seen hair like hers before. She was fine with it. If you mind that kind attention from people when you're not

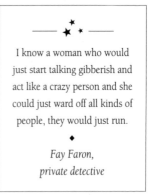

I know a woman who would just start talking gibberish and act like a crazy person and she could just ward off all kinds of people, they would just run.

♦

Fay Faron,
private detective

sure of what their motives are as they approach you, if that's going to bother you, I would take any real significant feature and downplay it. Put a hat on or whatever."

What about a worst case, I asked Lee. If you are physically attacked and you do not have a weapon, should you grab for sticks and rocks, even if you have no street fighting experience? The answer came without hesitation. "If you are at the point where you can no longer run and a physical battle is going to transpire, always use a weapon. Use any weapon at hand. A rock is fine. It extends anybody's capabilities. You don't have to be a rock-throwing artist to use a rock. Swing hard and aim for someplace where it would hurt. You can take somebody down with it. Don't worry about your attacker disarming you and using it against you. He can pick up a rock just as easily as you can, why does he need your rock? People I know who fight well, even good martial artists, adhere to the rule: if there is a weapon there, use it."

Animals offer a different challenge, warned Lee. Wild animals easily interpret an unknown human in their midst as a threat. "Never look a gorilla in the eyes," advised Lee. "Don't show your teeth to monkeys, they think it means you're going to bite them and they will bite you first. You can learn about specific wildlife for the regions you expect to visit." Lee says dogs the world over respond to the same general attitude. "Don't appear challenging, don't appear frightened and run. The best thing to do is keep going your own way and ignore them as much as possible. Don't stop and confront them. Without running, remove yourself as best you can. If it degenerates, pepper spray is pretty good on dogs. Climb a tree, pick up a rock. Dogs know what picking up a rock means. Many of them will then stop, not all of them."

Women traveling on business are probably at less risk than the backpacker, according to Lee, if only because they'll be in better hotels and riding in taxis instead of city buses. "On the other hand, you'll probably be carrying a two thousand dollar computer. The number one stolen items in the world right now are portable computers. You're advertising that you do have some money when you carry a computer. Try to put it in a bag that doesn't yell computer. Put it in a brown shopping bag instead of a nice flashy computer case with your initials on it. Be very careful about people following you to your hotel room, maybe not to get you but to burglarize the room once they understand you're carrying some valuable things with you. Computers and cameras are very valuable, and not just in Third World countries, in Los Angeles too."

Lee had another piece of advice for traveling business women that doesn't apply directly to physical safety, but certainly pertains to financial security. Watch out for a devious telephone scam based on phone companies that bill your telephone account for the time you spend calling a specific number. Here is how it works. The con artists manage to get your pager number, or your voice mail number. They page you overseas or leave you a voice mail and announce a number for you to call back. The number is outside of the United States, but the area code appears to be a U.S.-type. It is three digits and the number following it is seven digits, the same configuration as in the U.S. If you answer the page or message and call the number, the operator who answers tries to keep you on the line as long as possible, and the charges can be extraordinary, as high as fifty dollars a minute. Since the company is not in the U.S., it is not subject to U.S. regulations.

"What they do," Lee explained, "is buy a list of pager numbers, cell phone numbers, people with voice mail. They call and leave a very frantic message saying things like, 'Your husband is injured, call this number right away please!' or they'll put the call back number on your pager and leave 911 after it a few times. Then once you call you'll get put on hold and it can end up costing several hundred dollars if you don't successfully dispute the charges with the phone company that bills you."

Lee Lapin looked over the dessert menu one more time, decided against the chocolate truffles and the cheesecake, and got up from the table with a final warning. "Don't trust any deal that looks like it's too good to be true."

But don't worry too much about *foreign* surroundings. Remember these sobering domestic statistics from the U.S. Department of Justice: nearly 75 percent of sexual assault and rape victims say that their assailant was not a stranger.

Tips

➤ Guns, and even mace, are illegal in many destinations. But there are other methods for self protection. Consider learning a martial art. This will be a valuable tool while traveling, as well as at home. Remember that if you carry a weapon, it could be turned against you.

➤ Prepare yourself for the worst. Consider a rehearsal, with friends or in your mind, of an attack. Learn how you would react to a gun in your face or a knife at your throat. Survival courses that include simulated danger can be found through adult education schools in most metropolitan areas. These can include everything from judging body language to weapons training.

➤ Noise is effective. Practice screaming before you leave home. A healthy scream can scare an assailant, draw attention to your predicament, and bring help. Do not be afraid of making a scene.

➤ Loud whistles are another effective tool for scaring attackers and summoning aid. Consider wearing one as a necklace.

Just be sure that you can grab it easily. A noise-maker buried at the bottom of your purse is worthless if you have to dig for it during a crisis.

➤ As the characters in *Monty Python* suggest, if you are attacked, "Run away, run away, run away!"

➤ If you are attacked and decide to fight back, do everything you can to hurt your assailant. Aim for the eyes, solar plexus, and throat. Pull hair. Bite. Scratch. Remember the extreme vulnerability of a man's testicles. Grab and squeeze as hard as you can, as a woman I met in the desert once did. The man who was after her was hospitalized, never to bother her again. If possible, tear your attacker's clothing and other possessions to mark him for later police identification. Above all make noise, lots of excruciatingly loud noise.

➤ If you appear vulnerable to predators, you are more likely to be victimized.
Know your strengths and weaknesses. If you're out of shape, you're obviously going to be hard-pressed to outrun

I have a friend who takes a stun gun and pepper spray when she's hiking. She has another thing that beeps loudly and she keeps all these in her backpack. In a really dangerous situation she couldn't get them out fast enough to help herself. But, I think the city is more dangerous than walking in wilderness areas.

Much of it is attitude. As much as I travel alone, I've never had a problem. I don't do stupid things. When you watch those old horror movies where the woman goes into the basement alone in a strange house, well that's stupid.

◆

—*Casey Landry, businesswoman*

or fight off an attacker, so you may want to be more cautious than your marathon-running sister about bad neighborhoods and questionable circumstances.

➤ Be judicious about taking photographs. What may seem to you a simple tourist snapshot can be interpreted as a spy picture in some places. Stay safe by keeping your camera pointed away from military installations, airports, train stations, international border crossing points, and anyone in an official uniform. Even bridges and power generation plants are restricted for photographers by some oppressive governments. If you really want a picture of such things, seek specific approval from an authority you are convinced is in charge.

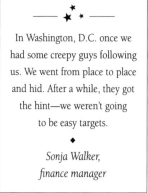

In Washington, D.C. once we had some creepy guys following us. We went from place to place and hid. After a while, they got the hint—we weren't going to be easy targets.

◆

Sonja Walker,
finance manager

➤ Binoculars also can be interpreted as spy paraphernalia by paranoid regimes. Avoid pointing your bird-watching glasses at army bases and police stations.

➤ Just as at home, elevators can be a vulnerable locale

We were walking in New York and someone said, "You shouldn't walk here," so I flagged down a policeman. He said, "Even I don't walk here," and he drove us home.

◆

Renate Moore,
retired

for a woman alone. If the door opens on a floor before yours and someone gets in who makes you feel uncomfortable, do not hesitate to get out. Similarly, do not get into an elevator if the passengers already inside seem at first glance like the wrong crowd. There's almost always an emergency button to ring.

➤ Be wary about riding alone in train compartments, especially at night. At the same time, balance that concern by choosing your compartment companions with care. Of course that requires snap decisions based on appearances, another reminder that your instincts are often your best protection.

➤ The U.S. State Department lists countries it considers dangerous for U.S. citizens and it is well worth checking with them to hear their latest warnings. These advisories are quite specific and could either help you avoid dangers or convince you to change your itinerary because of specific threats against women. For example, prior to the tragic highway robbery and rape in Guatemala of a group of Maryland college students, the State Department warned that "shootings, rapes, and

Sad, but true, I feel safe the minute I get out of America. Even if my purse is threatened my person is not.

♦

Susan L. Roth, children's book illustrator

violent assaults have for the most part occurred during daylight hours and in many cases have affected entire groups of American tourists. Highway travel has generally exposed visitors to increased risk of violent incident."

➤ Harassment is common for women travelers to Italy, especially in the south, as it is in other countries where *machismo* is a continuing cultural factor. Avoid sleeping in train stations and other public places where you could be vulnerable to assault, and do not count on the police to be free of the tendency to grope and fondle foreign women.

➤ It can be crucial to learn local customs and laws quickly. Watch your feet in Thailand where it is rude if they point at another, and be careful about touching the heads of other people—the head is respected as holy. Buddhist monks are not supposed to interact with women, so you should not touch or even be adjacent to them. Drug smuggling in Thailand, Malaysia, and some other Southeast Asian countries can result in the death penalty.

➤ Few countries are as inhospitable to single women as Saudi Arabia. If you go there it will not be as a tourist, no tourist visas are issued. It is illegal for women to drive rental cars. The sexes are segregated on city buses. Penalties for bringing pornography into the country are severe, and what might be considered by you to be a picture of a woman in a sexy outfit could well be considered to be pornography by Saudi customs officials.

I was flying into San Antonio and I had a layover in Dallas. It was late at night and this man just kept following me. It didn't dawn on me at first, but I'd go into the bookstore and he'd follow me. When I got on the plane, he did too and when I got off, he followed me to baggage claim and asked me where I was staying. The airport was deserted, so I walked over to a woman sitting in a booth for shuttle service and just stood right beside her. He finally went off to bother some other lone woman.

◆

*Jennifer Ricciuti,
technical trainer for
software design firm*

If you dress in what is considered immodest clothing in public places, you face abuse from the so-called religious police.

➤ If you enjoy a mane of luxurious hair—especially blond in countries where most women are dark-haired or cover their heads—it's an attention getter, and not always the type of attention you seek. One solution is to simply keep it tied back and covered.

➤ Are beautiful women more likely to attract unwanted attention than Plain Janes? Not necessarily. Their very attractiveness may help protect them because they might appear unapproachable. But this assumption is not foolproof protection, especially in the face of groups of men who may perceive the display of feminine beauty as immodest behavior.

➤ If the people don't scare you, the animals might. Without being paralyzed with paranoia, it is worthwhile to consider the potential dangers of animals in the road. We know a woman who travels with a pocketful of dog biscuits to pacify pariah strays. It's usually a good idea to avoid direct eye contact with any animal that appears threatening. A walking stick can provide you with a weapon against attack.

➤ For a complete listing of the types of deadly animals you can encounter while traveling, consult John "Lofty" Wiseman's book, *The SAS Urban Survival Handbook*. He tells stories about critters like the candiru, a skinny little South American catfish. The candiru is attracted by urine and likes to enter humans through urogenital body openings. The rear-pointing candiru spines cause great pain to the victim. "Wear tight protective clothing over genitalia," advises Lofty, "if tempted to bathe in suspect rivers and streams."

➤ Learn the psychology of scams and scam makers. They prey on the average person's reluctance to accuse another of wrong-doing, or even the intent to commit a crime. The same is true with purchasing scams. Whether it's trying to get you to buy mosaics in Agra, carpets in Morocco, shoes in Italy, or emeralds in Rio, there are some very clever people out there who are not actually criminals, but who are so skilled at manipulation they should be avoided.

➤ Fear can be your ally. This is the central theme of Gavin de Becker's book, *The Gift of Fear,* which was discussed in Chapter Three. If you walk into your hotel room and your things are not as you left them, then fear is an appropriate response and should motivate you to leave the room immediately and seek help. That sort of fear, based on a specific threat, is empowering, as opposed to the kind of generalized fear which is like phobias about the unknown.

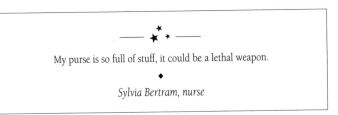

My purse is so full of stuff, it could be a lethal weapon.

◆

Sylvia Bertram, nurse

Chapter Thirteen

IF YOU BECOME
A VICTIM

I made a short cut for it and the next news was I was in a heap,
on a lot of spikes, some fifteen feet or so below ground level,
at the bottom of a bag-shaped game pit. It is at these times you
realize the blessing of a good thick skirt. Whereas, save for a
good many bruises, here I was with the fullness of my skirt tucked
under me, sitting on nine ebony spikes some twelve inches
long, in comparative comfort, howling lustily to be hauled out.

—*Mary Kingsley,* Travels in West Africa *(1897)*

———

*M*ay in Spain. For a birthday present, I find a three-week live-in Spanish language school on the Costa del Sol. Each day after the six hours of studying and eating, a group of us head down from our bucolic village to the public beach.

Hugo and Ines, who had studied at the same school the year before, warn us of the robberies they had heard about, especially near Malaga. Lock your car, they say, keep it in sight as much as you can.

One hot day we park our VW bus between the coast road and the dunes, and pile out for a nice spot on the sand. As is usually the case, I'm not much interested in swimming, going into water where tampons wash up on the shore as part of the flotsam. And fair as I am, I try to stay pretty covered up on the beach. So I sit in white clothes on a towel. But this day becomes just too hot even for my light summer whites.

"I'll be back in a minute or so," I say to Ines. "Please tell

Peter and Michael." They're playing Frisbee down the beach. Ines is topless and, as always, finds it funny that I keep my clothes on. "I'm going to the bus to change into my bathing suit."

I get into the bus, find something to eat, draw the curtains, eat and change. I stay only a few minutes and then carefully lock the sliding door before I head back to the beach and join the others—just out of sight over the dunes. Not more than a quarter hour later, we all are hungry and pack up our gear to head into town and buy food for dinner.

Peter gets into the driver's seat and immediately notices that the wing window on the passenger side is open. A quick look around and we see that the car has been ransacked. His suit is stolen. Binoculars, camera, tape recorder: gone. Michael's toys are still in the bus, along with some other more valuable things. Perhaps the thieves saw us coming and ran?

A break-in is a nasty violation of your personal space. After the initial shock of the

I had one bad experience in San Jose, Costa Rica. I was in a bus terminal, I had my brother with me and he went to get coffee. While I was waiting with my luggage somebody sat down next to me and said, are those your *colones*? That's their currency. I just looked and said no, and while I did that, someone from behind him had grabbed my backpack and run off with it. I yelled and the guy dropped my pack. Within two minutes, security was there.

◆

*Analou Sison,
finance manager*

I've traveled all over Europe and the only place anyone stuck a gun in my face was in California. My sister and I were robbed. I wanted to tell the guy to take the money. We were having such a good time. Maybe it's an illusion, but Europe feels safe to me.

◆

Mary Works, filmmaker

burglary sinks in, I remember how little time passed between me changing clothes alone in the bus—out of sight of Peter and the others—and the break-in. Whoever the bad guys were, they figured they were stealing from an empty car. But I was naked and alone in there.

We go to the police station, and the cops are blasé. "This happens all the time, especially to foreigners," the cop who fills out the report tells us. Our VW is equipped with California license plates. "Don't expect to get anything back," he says, "Don't expect us to catch them."

Lucky for us, our insurance covered the loss.

Crime is a potential problem in New York and New Delhi, in Austria and Australia. Victims of crimes anywhere often have a difficult time recovering from the emotional impact. But in a foreign country, especially if you are traveling alone, becoming a crime victim can be devastating. The American consulate can help you find counseling if you remain traumatized after a robbery or an attack. Fear can be an immobilizing emotion. It is important for you to reach out for help. You needn't be ashamed if you feel a need to return to familiar and safe surroundings. Going home should always be an alternative.

Tips

➤ If you are a robbery victim and you've followed the advice regarding copying your important papers, you'll be equipped with your credit card numbers, your passport numbers, and all the other crucial information you need to cancel service and obtain replacement cards and documents.

➤ Do not expect the local authorities to respond as the police do at home. Even in societies that seem on the surface to resemble ours, the rules are often quite different. In Mexico, for example, a serious traffic accident often results in both drivers being jailed for the duration of the investigation. Despite the inconvenience, consider doing without your own car and using public transport instead. In addition to eliminating driving stress, riding on buses and trains forces you into ideal opportunities for meeting the locals.

➢ If you become involved with a foreign criminal justice system—either as a victim of a crime or under suspicion of committing a crime—make every effort to get in touch with the U.S. embassy or closest consulate as soon as possible. The help you can expect varies from country to country, and depends on the specific government personnel you encounter. At the very least, you can probably count on them to contact your friends and relatives back home. Under emergency conditions, the U.S. government may advance you enough money to return home.

I've been mugged once and ironically it was in a parking lot in California after I got home from six weeks in Asia. My mother was scared for me the whole time I was there and yet I was perfectly safe. I got home and was mugged within a week.

I was walking through the parking lot at night and a guy called across to me, "Do you know what time it is?" Of course that's checking to see if you have a watch. I said, "No I don't have a watch on." Then he was in my face and said, "Give me that brooch." We scuffled and he grabbed it. He hit me in the mouth and I ran after him. He went across the freeway and I stopped. I have a scar on my face still to prove it.

◆

Fay Faron,
private detective

➤ The U.S. consulate will not recommend a lawyer if you run afoul of a foreign criminal justice system, but they will provide you with a list of lawyers available to represent you. Consular officers should visit with you periodically if you are held in custody, and should inform your friends and family back home about your status. Do not expect the U.S. government to come to your rescue unless your case is of political value to the current Administration.

➤ The best advice under most circumstances is to try to generate publicity about your predicament if you are facing some sort of criminal prosecution abroad. Most foreign governments do not want to generate worldwide negative publicity about their country and its policies, especially if tourism, as is increasingly the case, is important to their economies.

> One time I was taking a walk in Sofia, Bulgaria in a wonderful park. Some guy was following me and exposing himself. I walked faster and he walked faster. It was one of these wild parks and there weren't very many people around. So I finally got out of the park and went up to a door and knocked. I couldn't speak Bulgarian, but I let them know that I was frightened. The man took off.
>
> ♦
>
> *Karen Sandel,*
> *international consultant*

➤ Within the U.S., your AAA or other automobile club card may be used instead of bail in many jurisdictions. Check with your club for details of what they offer where. Your card also may be valuable at foreign clubs for maps and other services.

It was probably around 7:30 when I left the Paris apartment. When the train arrived, I foolishly got into a car that was otherwise unoccupied. I heard the door to the compartment behind me open. I was sitting there when suddenly someone grabbed my breast from behind. Rage, I tell you, absolute rage filled my heart, and I jumped up to face a young man about my size. I immediately positioned myself in the most basic self-defense pose—a semi-crouch with both hands positioned in front of me—and I yelled NOOO!! as loud as I possibly could right in his face.

This startled him for a moment and he backed up. At that moment some more people came into our car, and he sat down in the back of the car. I moved into the next car. When we got to my stop, I exited the train, and so did he. It was very crowded, and he didn't try to approach me. But he made some lewd faces and some general French gutter talk followed, as we went our separate ways.

♦

Jenny Teaford, publicist

Chapter Fourteen

COPING WITH FEAR:
ONE WOMAN'S STORY

Danger: exposure or vulnerability to harm or evil; risk; peril

—*The American Heritage Dictionary*

———

*T*he following story by Rebecca Aaland will be familiar to many women in its theme, if not its place: the author walks the razor edge between crippling paranoia and intuition-fueled fear. Rebecca lives in San Francisco with her husband, Mikkel, and their daughter, Miranda. Her story "The Nature of Birth" appeared in *Travelers' Tales: Women in the Wild*.

A Stroll on the Beach

It was fall, and there was a distinct coldness to the air. A communal taxi had dropped me off in Tabarqa, on the northern coast of Tunisia near the Algerian border. The only transportation onwards left the next morning. Late that afternoon I decided to walk on the empty beach alone. I walked east out of the town, up into deserted sand dunes overlooking the ocean, white from the rolling surf. After a time I became aware of a figure in the distance, dark against the sand. I kept walking, and so did he. I realized he was following me, and fear sent a rush of adrenaline through me.

Why should I be afraid? In Egypt I had gone alone with a

man to eat a meal on the roof of his family's house, trusting my intuition that the hospitality extended was genuine. In Morocco at the edge of the Sahara I let a border guard take me under his wing when the Algerians sent me back across the remote border crossing on foot. Such encounters based on trust have provided me with good reason to have faith in humankind.

Yet now my intuition told me there was danger. I veered down towards the water. There was no one else, just him, still at a distance but following, and me. It was my refusal to succumb to the fear of being a woman traveling alone which led me out to the beach in the first place. Now I was confronted with that fear in a tangible form, an unknown man following me. My heart raced and I felt hunted. How much of my sense of danger was appropriate, and how much was simply baggage I brought with me, fear of the unknown in the face of the foreign? I wanted to walk on, ignoring my fear. I wanted to feel free where I was, and I wanted to trust the world around me.

In the West Bank near Jerusalem I had been jumped by a gang of young boys. I was crossing a grassy hillside when they appeared out of nowhere and threw me to the ground, pounding me with large rocks they held and grabbing my crotch and breasts. I did not want to carry the fear and pain of that encounter with me on other travels, and so I walked out on that Tunisian beach when the sound of the waves invited. Fear can rob any experience of its joy, and can strip travel of what I most value, connectedness. Fear seemed to me only a sad reminder of my potential vulnerability, and a wall between me and the world I wanted to observe and experience.

As I walked on my fear became overwhelming and physical. This was not a matter of trusting in a person. The only reason I didn't want to turn around was precisely the reason why I felt I needed to—I was a woman and alone. In North Africa I constantly felt a need to prove to myself that I was fearless and comfortable in the public world of men. I thought a real traveler took risks and had courage. I struggled between the fear in my body and the stubbornness in my mind.

My body was stiff as I turned to walk back towards town. He turned as well, at first staying in the dunes, but then cutting down to the beach and closing some of the distance between us. I forced myself to walk at a steady pace, all my senses trained on him, although the only way to be sure where he was was to stop and look out at the waves, and catch a glimpse of him out of the corner of my eye. He was close enough now for me to tell he was young, but not close enough to tell the details of his face. I kept walking.

I could see the town now, coming closer with each step. The growing proximity of the buildings reassured me, even though the streets seemed deserted. The next time I looked back he was gone.

It is clear to me now that to accept my fear was to honor my instincts and to accept the world as it is, rather than how I wished it to be. Risk is inherent in travel, which is part of its allure, but senseless risk makes no more sense traveling than it does at home, and no more sense for a woman than for a man. Turning around on the beach that afternoon was not an act of turning my back on a culture, as I thought it was. I did what I would do anywhere, accepting that the world is not a safe theme park, but rather a place of real difference, mystery and sometimes danger. There was no way for me to know whether on that beach he followed me with malice, or to observe that which was foreign, or perhaps even to protect me. What I do know is what I most remember is my fear, and that I did not relax until I reached my hotel.

Epilogue

RISK AND REWARD

What, after all, is adventure but
inconvenience properly regarded?

—*G.K. Chesterton*

———

*S*afety and security mean taking care of yourself in all ways. You want to feel as good about yourself on the road as you do at home. After all, it's your trip.

I'm not a paranoid traveler, and most of the situations we point out in this book won't happen to you. I've traveled all over the world, from the wilderness to the cities, alone and with others. My overall experiences and memories are spectacular.

For his work as a news reporter, Peter travels to some of the most dangerous places and situations in the world, and some of the survival tactics he's learned and uses are incorporated into this book because they can be of crucial value for those of us who do not seek out dangerous destinations. I expect the best and usually enjoy the best that traveling offers. But being aware and careful is valuable protection no matter where you go.

Over the years I've traveled, the ideas of safety and security have become so integrated with my routines in my mind that they're automatic—much like locking the door at home. But instinct and awareness always plays the biggest role, and paranoia almost none. To be careful and open is a delicate balance—

finding the place where you feel comfortable for whatever level of adventure you want.

Most women have experienced—traveling or at home—a certain vulnerability perceived by almost all cultures as unique to our gender. Even my sons, who know me as a capable, strong, and healthy woman, sometimes act as protectors in situations I have handled alone all my life. Traveling with them as children, I was their protector. As adult men, perhaps they have caught the universal message that many women become victims. Perhaps they consider me too trusting.

Many of my women friends echo my philosophy: intuition and instinct are the best protectors for a woman. Each woman knows her own limits and knows that there is always an element of danger in travel. Risks can be reduced with attention, preparation, and awareness. Knowing dangers and devices for protecting yourself enables you to screen your risks when you can, and reduce or survive them when you can't.

May you have a wonderful and carefree trip.

RESOURCES AND REFERENCES

—

Books, Magazines, and Newsletters

A few books about women traveling to consider while on the road, or before you leave.

Anthologies and Travelogues

Bond, Marybeth, ed. *Travelers Tales: A Woman's World.* San Francisco: Travelers' Tales, Inc., 1995. Awarded the Lowell Thomas Gold Medal Award from the Society of American Travel Writers for Best Travel Book. An eloquent collection of women's stories that will move you out of your armchair and take you along paths lined with memory, the spirit of adventure, and the strength of womanhood.

Bond, Marybeth and Pamela Michael, eds. *Travelers' Tales: A Mother's World.* San Francisco: Travelers' Tales, Inc., 1998. A collection that illuminates and celebrates what it means to be a mother on the road.

Jansz, Natania and Miranda Davies, eds. *More Women Travel: Adventures and Advice from More Than 60 Countries.* London:

Rough Guides, 1995. Anthology with useful notes at the end
of each tale, offering a listing of special problems women may
encounter in the country where the story took place.

Jansz, Natania and Miranda Davies, eds. *Women Travel: A Rough
Guide Special.* London: Rough Guides, 1990.

Laqueur, Walter, ed. *The Terrorism Reader: A Historical Anthology*.
New Jersey: New American Library. A unique anthology that
brings together the most notable proponents, critics, and
analysts of terrorism from ancient times to today.

Laufer, Peter. *Nightmare Abroad: Stories of Americans Imprisoned
in Foreign Lands.* San Francisco: Mercury House, 1993. The
result of research that took Peter around the world to dozens
of countries where he learned about the plight of Americans
in jails, many of whom are women.

McCauley, Lucy, ed. *Women in the Wild: True Stories of Adventure
and Connection.* San Francisco: Travelers' Tales, Inc., 1998. A
collection of women's travel stories as they foray into the
wilderness and visit Mother Nature.

Morris, Mary and Larry O'Connor, eds. *Maiden Voyages:
Writings of Women Travelers.* New York: Vintage Departures,
1993. A collection of stories, old and new, by and for women.

Morris, Mary. *Nothing to Declare: Memoirs of a Woman Traveling
Alone.* New York: Houghton Mifflin, 1988. A travelogue and
journey into the self as she relates the realities of place, poverty,
and machismo of Mexico.

Rogers, Susan Fox, ed. *Solo: On Her Own Adventure*. Seattle: Seal Press, 1996. A collection of 26 inspiriting stories by women who describe the challenges and exhilarating rewards of going it alone.

Rogers, Susan Fox, ed. *Another Wilderness: New Outdoor Writing by Women*. Seattle: Seal Press, 1994. A compelling collection of outdoor stories by women.

Advice and Reference Books

Axtel, Roger E., ed. *Do's and Taboos Around the World*. New York: John Wiley & Sons, 1993.

Benjamin, Meda and Andrea Freedman. *The Peace Corps and More: 120 Ways to Work, Study and Travel in the Third World*. Carson, California: Seven Locks Press, Inc., 1989.

Bezruchka, Stephen. *The Pocket Doctor: Your Ticket to Good Health While Traveling*. Seattle: Mountaineers Books, 1992.

Bond, Marybeth. *Gutsy Mamas: Travel Tips and Wisdom for Mothers on the Road*. San Francisco: Travelers' Tales, Inc., 1998. Indispensible pocket guide full of tips and roadworthy wisdom.

Bond, Marybeth. *Gusty Women: Travel Tips and Wisdom for the Road*. San Francisco: Travelers' Tales Inc., 1996. A pocket guide containing funny, instructive, inspiring travel vignettes and tips for novice and experienced travelers.

Brewer, James D. *The Danger from Strangers: Confronting the Threat of Assault.* New York: Plenum Press, 1994.

Brownmiller, Susan. *Against Our Will.* New York: Simon & Schuster, 1975. The classic on rape that can help women prepare to guard against sexual assault on the road.

Buchwald, Emilie, Pamela Fletcher, and Martha Roth, eds. *Transforming a Rape Culture.* Minneapolis: Milkweed Editions, 1993. An anthology of articles on rape.

Cummings, Stephen M.D. and Dana Ullman, M.P.H. Everybody's *Guide to Homeopathic Medicines.* New York: Jeremy P. Tarcher/Putnam Books, 1991.

de Becker, Gavin. *The Gift of Fear.* New York: Dell, 1997. Compendium of priceless ideas and experiences directing women to understand and recognize their natural instincts for danger.

Devine, Elizabeth and Nancy L. Braganti. *The Travelers' Guide to Asian Customs and Manners.* New York: St. Martin's Press, 1986.

Fisher, Frederick. *Culture Shock: Successful Traveling Abroad.* Portland: Graphic Arts Center Publishing, 1995. Contains intriguing survival tactics for retirees as well as the general population.

McMillon, Bill. *Volunteer Vacations: A Directory of Short Term Adventures That Will Benefit You and Others* . Chicago: Chicago Review Press, 1995.

Moss, Maggie and Gemma Moss. *Handbook for Women Travellers*. London: Judy Platkus Publishers, 1995. Collection of tips along with tales of woe and successful traveling from over 100 of their friends.

Panos, Maesimund B. M.D. and Jane Heimlich. *Homeopathic Medicine at Home*. New York: J.P. Tarcher, 1980.

Pelton, Robert Young, Coskun Aval, and Wink Dulles. *Fielding's The World's Most Dangerous Places*. Redondo Beach, California: Fielding Worldwide, 1998.

Schroeder, Dirk. *Staying Healthy in Asia Africa, and Latin America*. Chico, California: Moon Publications, 1993.

Sterling, Richard. *The Fearless Diner: Travel Tips and Wisdom for Eating Around the World*. San Francisco: Travelers' Tales., Inc. 1997. A pocket primer on world gastronomy which incorporates essay, anecdote, and voices of experience to guide the reader through the realm of adventure eating.

Strong, Sanford. *Strong on Defense: Survival Rules to Protect You and Your Family from Crime*. New York: Simon & Schuster, Inc. Valuable techniques and precautions that can be used to protect yourself in any situation.

Strong, Sanford. *Strong Against Crime* (video). Available through Ladies Home Journal, Resources, Dept. L0997, POB 9381, Des Moines, IA 50306. 800-763-6393.

.rong, Sanford. *Strong Kids Against Crime* (video). Available through Ladies Home Journal, Resources, Dept. L0997, POB 9381, Des Moines, IA 50306. 800-763-6393.

Survival. Department of the Army field manual available in government book stores. Offers practical advice for far-flung adventurers and step-by-step procedures for navigating, finding water, even slaughtering and preparing wildlife.

Warshaw, Robin. *I Never Called it Rape.* New York: Ms. Foundation, 1988. The *Ms.* magazine report on recognizing, fighting, and surviving date and acquaintance rape.

Wiseman, John "Lofty". *The SAS Urban Survival Handbook.* London: HarperCollins UK, 1996.

Wilson-Howarth, Jane. *Healthy Travel: Bugs, Bites & Bowels.* London: Cadogan Guides, 1995.

Windsor, Natalie. *The Safe Tourist.* Los Angeles: Corkscrew Press, 1995. A collection of useful tips in checklist form.

Zepatos, Thalia. *A Journey of One's Own: Uncommon Advice for the Independent Woman Traveler.* Portland, Oregon: Eighth Mountain Press, 1992.

Travel Newsletters and Magazines

How to Get Anything on Anybody—The Newsletter
Periodic newsletter published by a security expert based on the format of the book by the same name. Website catalog of related

products available at: www.intelligence.to
Intelligence Incorporated
3555 S. El Camino Real
San Mateo, CA 94403

Journeywoman
Quarterly women's travel magazine
50 Prince Arthur Avenue Suite 1703
Toronto, Ontario M5R 1B5, Canada
416-929-7654

Maiden Voyages
Quarterly literary magazine & guide to women's travel
109 Minna Street, Suite 240
San Francisco, CA 94105
510-528-8425

Transitions Abroad
Monthly magazine and resource guide to educational and work
opportunities abroad
Dept. TRA, Box 300
Denville, NJ 07834
800-293-0373

Travel Matters
Complimentary newsletter
Moon Publications
P.O. Box 3040
Chico, CA 95927
800-345-5473

Services and Organizations

Mail Order Companies

Travelsmith
In addition to travel-related equipment, Travelsmith offers a service with live operators with advice on what to bring where, weather, and other travel-related questions.
Catalogue: 800-950-1600
Travel line: 800-995-7010

Magellans
Travel-related equipment. Also maintains a website at:
www.magellans.com
Catalogue: 800-962-4943

High Street Emporium
Intriguing and unique specialty travel items, including the EVAC-U-8 Smoke Hood, are available from this general interest catalog.
Catalogue: 800-362-5500

Austin House
Specializes in electric and telephone plug adapters. Their amazingly complete stock includes items for virtually every country on the planet.
Pamphlet: 800-268-5157

Organizations Specializing in Women's Travel

Above the Clouds Trekking
P.O. Box 398 E
Worcester, MA 01602
800-233-4499

Adventure Associates
P.O. Box 16304
Seattle, WA 98116
206-932-8352

Backcountry
P.O. Box 4029
Bozeman, MT 59772
800-575-1540

Backroads
1516 Fifth Street
Berkeley, CA 94710-1740
800-462-2848

Becoming An Outdoorswoman
College of Natural Resources
University of Wisconsin, ST
Stevens Point, WI 54481-3897
715-346-2853

Call of the Wild
2519 Cedar Street
Berkeley, CA 94708
510-849-9292

Great Old Broads for Wilderness
1942 Broadway, Suite 206
Boulder, CO 80302
303-443-7024

Inca Floats
1311 63rd Street
Emeryville, CA 94608
510-420-1550

International Expeditions
1 Environs Park
Helena, AL 35080
800-633-4734

Journeys
4011 Jackson
Ann Arbor, MI 48103
800-255-8735

Mariah Wilderness Expeditions
P.O. Box 248
Point Richmond, CA 94807
415-233-2303

Mountain Travel/Sobek
6420 Fairmont Avenue
El Cerrito, CA 94530-3606
800-227-2384

Myths & Mountains
976 Tee Court
Incline Village, NV 89451
800-670-6984

Natural Habitat Adventures
2945 Center Green Court
Boulder, CO 80301
800-543-8917

Nature Expeditions International
6400 East El Dorado Circle, Suite 210
Tucson, AZ 85715
800-869-0639

Overseas Adventure Travel
625 Mount Auburn Street
Cambridge, MA 02138
800-221-0814

Rainbow Adventures
15033 Kelly Canyon Road
Bozeman, MT 59715
800-804-8686

Roots & Wings Excursions
Travel Adventures for Mothers & Daughters
423 Carlisle Drive, Suite A
Herndon, VA 20170
800-722-9005, 303-443-7024

Sheri Griffith Expeditions
P.O. Box 1324
Moab, UT 84532
800-332-2439

Top Guides
1825 San Lorenzo Avenue
Berkeley, CA 94707
800-867-6777

Turtle Tours, Inc.
Box 1147/Dept ES
Carefree, AZ 85377
602-488-3688

Wild Women Adventures
107 N. Main Street
Sebastopol, CA 95472
800-992-1322

Wilderness Travel
801 Allston Way
Berkeley, CA 94710
800-368-2794

Womenship
410 Severn Avenue
The Boathouse
Annapolis, MD 21403
800-342-9295

Women's Travel Club
21401 NE 38th Avenue
Aventura, FL 33180
800-480-4448/305-936-9669

Womentours
Bicycle Tours for Women
P.O. Box 931
Driggs, ID 83422
800-247-1444

Lesbian Travel

Gay & Lesbian Travel Specialists Network
2300 Market Street, Suite 142
San Francisco, CA 94114
415-552-5140

International Gay Travel Association
P.O. Box 4972
Key West, FL 33041
303-294-5135

Olivia Records and Lesbian Travel
4400 Market Street
Oakland, CA 94608
800-631-6277/510-655-0364

House Swaps and Homestays

American-International Homestays, Inc.
P.O. Box 7178
Boulder, CO 80306
800-876-2048

Experiment in International Living Federation
P.O. Box 595
Putney, VT 05346
802-387-4210

Friendship Force
57 Forsyth Street NW, Suite 900
Atlanta, GA 30303
404-522-9490

House Exchange Program
952 Virginia Ave.
Lancaster, PA 17603
717-393-8985

Intervac/International Home Exchange
P.O. Box 59054
San Francisco, CA 94519
415-435-3497

Interhome
124 Little Falls Road
Fairfield, NJ 07004
201-882-6864

LEX Exchange/LEX America
68 Leonard Street
Belmont, MA 02178
617-489-5800

U.S. Servas
11 John Street #407
New York, NY 10038
212-267-0252

Vacation Exchange Club
P.O. Box 820
Hale'iwa, HI 96712
800-638-3841

Villas & Apartments Abroad, Ltd.
420 Madison Avenue
New York, NY 10017
212-759-1025

Women Welcome Women
c/o Joan Beyette
11215 26th Street SW
Calgary, Alberta T2W 5C6, CANADA

Reference and Research

CDC—Centers for Disease Control
Maintains current specific health warnings filed by region.
888-232-3228
888-232-3299 (phone line to request written information to be sent via fax)
Website: www.cdc.gov

Homeopathic Educational Services
Mail order house with catalog of homeopathic
books, remedies, travel and home kits
2124 Kittredge St.
Berkeley, CA 94704
800-835-9051

International Association for Medical Assistance to Travelers
Worldwide directory of English-speaking doctors.
716-754-4883

Peters Projection World Map
Friendship Press
P.O. Box 37844
Cincinnati, OH 45222

U.S. State Department
Prepares citizen warnings for particularly dangerous locales.
Recorded announcements of those crisis zones.
202-647-5225
202-647-6201 (to arrange for fax copies of warnings)
Website: http://travel.state.gov

Fear of Flying

Fearless Flyer Classes
American Airlines
800-451-5106

Freedom from Fear of Flying, Inc.
2021 Country Club Prado
Coral Gables, FL 33134

Pegasus Fear of Flying Foundation
200 Eganfuskee Street
Jupiter, FL 33477-5068
800-FEAR-NOT

World Wide Web Resources

Search the World Wide Web under "Travel Safety" or "Women, Travel" or point your browser to the following sites:

Access-Able Travel Source: http://www.access-able.com/

Centers For Disease Control:
http://www.cdc.gov/travel/travel.html

Embassies and Consulates:
http://www.embassy.org/embassies/eep-1100.html

Foreign Commonwealth Office's Travel Advice:
http://www.fco.gov.uk/travel/default.asp

International Association for Medical Assistance to Travelers:
http://www.sentex.net/~iamat/index.html

Lonely Planet's The Scoop and Postcards: www.lonelyplanet.com

National Transportation Safety Board: http://www.ntsb.gov/

Overseas Security Advisory Council: http://ds.state.gov/osac-menu.cfm

Smart Date: http://www.smartdate.com/

Tourism Offices Worldwide Directory:
http://www.mbnet.mb.ca/lucas/travel/tourism-offices.html

Travel Health Information Service: http://travelhealth.com/

Travel Safety from Safe Within: http://www.safewithin.com/travelsafe/travel.resource.html

U.S. State Department Travel Warnings & Consular Information Sheets: http://travel.state.gov/travel_warnings.html

Vapor Trails' Tips & Resources:
http://www.vaportrails.com/Resources/resourcesf4.html

World Health Organization: http://www.who.int/

Miscellaneous Resources

Credit Card Advice

American Express
U.S.   800-528-4800
Abroad   910-333-321 collect

Diner's Club
U.S.   800-346-3779
Abroad   303-790-2433 collect

Discover
U.S.   800-347-2683
Abroad   not accepted

Mastercard
U.S.   800-622-7747
Abroad   303-278-8000 collect

Visa
U.S.   800-336-8472
Abroad   410-581-7931 collect

Travelers' Check Advice

American Express
U.S.   800-221-7282
Abroad   offices worldwide

Bank of America
U.S.   800-227-6811
Abroad   410-581-5353 collect

Citicorp
U.S.   800-645-6556
Abroad   813-623-1709 collect

Thomas Cook
U.S.   800-223-7373
Abroad   609-987-7300 collect

Visa
U.S.   800-227-6811/800-732-1322
Abroad   44-173-331-8949 collect

LIST OF
CONTRIBUTORS

———

ABOUT THE AUTHORS

───

Sheila Swan Laufer has been traveling the world for fun and business since the 1960s. From camping in Latin America to luxury resorts in the Old World, from long-distance buses across the American South to first-class airliner seats five miles high, from quaint pensions on the Iberian Peninsula to five-star hotels in Oceana, she has experienced the extremes travel offers—taking notes all along the way.

Peter Laufer is an award-winning journalist whose career has taken him to many of the world's most dangerous destinations. While researching his book *Nightmare Abroad*, he traveled around the world, stopping in twenty-one countries, interviewing Americans locked up in foreign prisons. Another of his books, *Iron Curtain Rising*, recounts his journey through Eastern Europe during the revolutions of 1989–1990.

Together the two wrote and photographed *Neon Nevada*, a study of the impact of the neon sign on Nevada culture, published by the University of Nevada Press.

NOTES

NOTES

NOTES

NOTES

NOTES

NOTES

_____

_____

_____

_____

_____

_____

_____

_____

_____

_____

_____

_____

_____

_____

_____

_____

_____

_____

_____

NOTES

NOTES

NOTES

NOTES

NOTES

NOTES

TRAVELERS' TALES GUIDES

LOOK FOR THESE TITLES IN THE SERIES

✐PECIAL INTEREST

THE GIFT OF TRAVEL
THE BEST OF TRAVELERS' TALES
Edited by Larry Habegger, James O'Reilly & Sean O'Reilly
ISBN 1-885211-25-2, 240 pages, $14.95

THERE'S NO TOILET PAPER ON THE ROAD LESS TRAVELED
THE BEST OF TRAVEL HUMOR AND MISADVENTURE
Edited by Doug Lansky
ISBN 1-885211-27-9, 190 pages, $12.95

LOVE & ROMANCE
TRUE STORIES OF PASSION ON THE ROAD
Edited by Judith Babcock Wylie
ISBN 1-885211-18-X, 318 pages, $17.95

A DOG'S WORLD
TRUE STORIES OF MAN'S BEST FRIEND ON THE ROAD
Edited by Christine Hunsicker
232 pages, ISBN 1-885211-23-6, $12.95

$\mathcal{W}$OMEN'S TRAVEL

WOMEN IN THE WILD
TRUE STORIES OF ADVENTURE AND CONNECTION
Edited by Lucy McCauley
ISBN 1-885211-21-X, 307 pages, $17.95

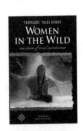

A MOTHER'S WORLD
JOURNEYS OF THE HEART
Edited by Marybeth Bond & Pamela Michael
234 pages, ISBN 1-885211-26-0, $14.95

———— ★ ★ ★ ————

Winner of the Lowell Thomas Award for Best Travel Book—Society of American Travel Writers

A WOMAN'S WORLD
TRUE STORIES OF LIFE ON THE ROAD
Edited by Marybeth Bond
ISBN 1-885211-06-6
475 pages, $17.95

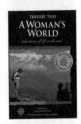

GUTSY WOMEN
TRAVEL TIPS AND WISDOM FOR THE ROAD
By Marybeth Bond
ISBN 1-885211-15-5, 124 pages, $7.95

GUTSY MAMAS
TRAVEL TIPS AND WISDOM FOR MOTHERS ON THE ROAD
By Marybeth Bond
ISBN 1-885211-20-1, 148 pages, $7.95

ℬODY & SOUL

THE ROAD WITHIN
TRUE STORIES OF
TRANSFORMATION AND THE SOUL
*Edited by Sean O'Reilly, James O'Reilly
& Tim O'Reilly*
ISBN 1-885211-19-8, 464 pages, $17.95

*Small Press Book
Award Winner and
Benjamin Franklin
Award Finalist*

FOOD
A TASTE OF THE ROAD
*Edited by Richard Sterling,
Introduction by Margo True
ISBN 1-885211-09-0
444 pages, $17.95*

*Silver Medal Winner of the
Lowell Thomas Award for
Best Travel Book—Society of
American Travel Writers*

THE FEARLESS DINER
TRAVEL TIPS AND WISDOM FOR EATING
AROUND THE WORLD
*By Richard Sterling
ISBN 1-885211-22-8, 139 pages, $7.95*

COUNTRY GUIDES

ITALY

Edited by Anne Calcagno
Introduction by Jan Morris
ISBN 1-885211-16-3, 463 pages, $17.95

FRANCE

Edited by James O'Reilly, Larry Habegger
& Sean O'Reilly
ISBN 1-885211-02-3, 432 pages, $17.95

MEXICO

Edited by James O'Reilly & Larry Habegger
ISBN 1-885211-00-7, 426 pages, $17.95

SPAIN

Edited by Lucy McCauley
ISBN 1-885211-07-4, 495 pages, $17.95

COUNTRY GUIDES

THAILAND

*Edited by James O'Reilly
& Larry Habegger
ISBN 1-885211-05-8
483 pages, $17.95*

—————— ★ ★ ★ ——————

***Winner of the Lowell Thomas
Award for Best Travel
Book—Society of American
Travel Writers***

BRAZIL

*Edited by Annette Haddad & Scott Doggett
Introduction by Alex Shoumatoff
ISBN 1-885211-11-2, 433 pages, $17.95*

NEPAL

*Edited by Rajendra S. Khadka
ISBN 1-885211-14-7, 423 pages, $17.95*

INDIA

*Edited by James O'Reilly & Larry Habegger
ISBN 1-885211-01-5, 477 pages, $17.95*

ℭITY GUIDES

HONG KONG
Edited by James O'Reilly, Larry Habegger & Sean O'Reilly
ISBN 1-885211-03-1, 438 pages, $17.95

PARIS
Edited by James O'Reilly, Larry Habegger & Sean O'Reilly
ISBN 1-885211-10-4, 424 pages, $17.95

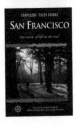

SAN FRANCISCO
Edited by James O'Reilly, Larry Habegger & Sean O'Reilly
ISBN 1-885211-08-2, 432 pages, $17.95

....

SUBMIT YOUR OWN TRAVEL TALE

Do you have a tale of your own that you would like to submit to Travelers' Tales? We highly recommend that you first read one or more of our books to get a feel for the kind of story we're looking for. For submission guidelines and a list of titles in the works, send a SASE to:

Travelers' Tales Submission Guidelines
P.O. Box 610160, Redwood City, CA 94061

or send email to ***ttguidelines@online.oreilly.com***
or visit our web site at **www.oreilly.com/ttales**

You can send your story to the address above or via email to ***ttsubmit@oreilly.com***. On the outside of the envelope, ***please indicate what country/topic your story is about***. If your story is selected for one of our titles, we will contact you about rights and payment.

We hope to hear from you. In the meantime, enjoy the stories!